ANNABELLE'S BABY

Annabelle's Baby

Ann Capozzoli

Copyright © 2023 by Ann Capozzoli

All rights reserved. No part of this publication may be reproduced, distributed, or transmitted in any form or by any means, including photocopying, recording, or other electronic or mechanical methods, without the prior written permission of the copyright owner or the publisher, except in the case of brief quotations embodied in critical reviews and certain other noncommercial uses permitted by copyright law. For permission requests, write to the publisher, addressed "Attention: Permissions Coordinator," at the address below.

ARPress
45 Dan Road Suite 5
Canton MA 02021
Hotline: 1(888) 821-0229
Fax: 1(508) 545-7580

Ordering Information:
Quantity sales. Special discounts are available on quantity purchases by corporations, associations, and others. For details, contact the publisher at the address above.

Printed in the United States of America.

ISBN-13:	Softcover	979-8-89330-509-8
	eBook	979-8-89330-511-1
	Hardback	979-8-89330-510-4

Library of Congress Control Number: 2024900474

Table of Contents

Part I : Westfield, NJ

Yellow 1
Lee 4
He Hardly Ever Called 7
Rhonda Tiger 9
Do You Love Me? 10
Navy Blue Skirt 11
See You at C.U. 14
Dr. Tyndall 18
Bitter Forfeit 21
Catholic Charities 23
Tuna Casserole 25
A Bathing Suit with a Skirt 27
A Craving for Liverwurst 29
Bubbles in My Belly 30
Pills for Depression 32
The Psychiatrist 33
The Boraks 35
Giggles 38
The Sculptor 39
Is This Therapy? 41
I Couldn't Say No 43

Hopeless 45

I Didn't Last Long at the Boraks 46

The Hungarian Couple 48

Yellow Cottage 51

Thanksgiving Dinner 53

Heart Burn 55

Sunday's Child 57

Anthony of Padua 59

The Old School 60

Pink Pills 62

Back in Westfield 64

Don't Look at Him That Way 65

The Book Bag 67

Tons of Fun 69

The Newman Club 71

Father Murphy and Father Flanagan 72

In God's Hands 74

A Proper Baptism 76

The Newman Club Retreat 78

Part II : Brooklyn, NY

Everybody Knew 82

Pursuit 84

Did I Love Erik? 85

Lawrence Welk 87

Chi Chi 88

Dante and Beatrice 89
The Blues 91
Ding Dong 93
But **Why** Do You Love Me? 96
Proposal in the Subway Station 98
Those Scandinavians 99
Thursday 101
S. Klein on the Square 103
A Family 104
Where Are the Flowers? 105
My Father 107
My Mother 108
Helen 109
The "Reception" 110
A Cup of Coffee and a Snack 111
The Gold Cross 113
How Could You Not Like Dogs? 114
I Hate it When You Sing 115
How Could I Know I was Pregnant? 117
Baby Grand Piano 118
Fried Shit 120
Staten Island 121
Willoughby Avenue 122
Lethargy 123
What Fun! 124
Mrs. Rosenberg 126
Why I decided I liked Pete Sultanis 128

My Mother-in-law, My Idol	130
Martini Time	132
Madman Behind the Wheel	134
A Name for the Baby	136
Perfect	137
No Comb	139
Dan's Theory	140
Rag Doll	141
Tony's Nose	143
A Red Crib	144
Marjory Kleinman	146
Olive Wamsley	148
Corina Williams	150
Saundra	152
House Party	153
African Side-Neck	154
I'm Your Mommy	156
Oh, Jill!	158
Jill	160
The Red Brick Apartment Building	161
The Film	163
Doug's Drugs	165
Advice From Joan	169
Ashamed	170
Leonard Schutz	171
Mr. Schutz Meets My Father	174
Bad Girl	176

Psychologists Made My Mother Cry 177
Mr. Schutz Meets Erik...179
Martha 181
Sorting Things Out 183

Part III : Kingston, NY

Tough..185
Divorce Papers 187
Divorce 188
Adoption 190
Not That Bad 192
I Still Cry 193
Biological Mother 194
Why do I Still Cry? 196

To Russell Thorpe, my beloved husband, without whose gentle coaxing these pages would never have seen the light of day.

Part I

Westfield, NJ

Yellow

My parents, my younger sister and I sit at the table in our yellow kitchen in Westfield. In my mother's mind yellow is the color you paint a kitchen. Yellow is the color of the chintz you buy to make the curtains. Yellow is the color of the chair cushions, the plastic table cloth.

My mother has recently rearranged the kitchen furniture. My father, who sits at the head of the table, is now directly under a shelf.

We have just finished dinner and are having dessert. I am seventeen and everything my parents do annoys me. Right now they annoy me with the sounds they make drinking coffee. My mother gulps. My father slurps.

Slurp, gulp, slurp.

My father lectures me about boyfriends. Why can't I go out with a nice Catholic boy? A nice Catholic Italian boy? Why can't I go out during the daytime with a nice Catholic Italian boy? Why always at night with these Protestant boys? Am I looking for trouble? What's wrong with a nice Catholic boy? A nice Italian boy?

My father looks at me, his eyes big and wide, his black eyebrows raised, his forehead raked with lines arching up beyond the point where he once had hair. He makes me sick. The sight of him. The sounds of him.

"From now on, no more dates at night. Tell your boyfriends to take you to the matinee."

I pick up a chocolate cookie from the plate in front of me – *Happy Family Assortment* is the brand my mother buys for us. "If the last boy on earth was Italian, I'd never go out with him!" I yell as I throw the cookie at my father, hitting his forehead.

He scrapes back his chair and stands up in one quick, angry motion.

I hear the bang of his head against the shelf as he rises and I spring from my chair – I'm in big trouble now. I push past my sister, circle around my mother, bolt through the kitchen doorway into the living room and round the corner to the stairs. If I can scramble up the stairs to my room before my raging father catches me, I might be able to hold the door shut against him.

But before I reach the stairs, he grabs my shoulder, spins me around and hurls me against the wall. "What did you say to me? You think you can talk to *me* that way?"

Does he expect an answer?

I've sunk down the wall. I am curled on the floor. My arms protect my head, my body is bent forward, my knees cover my breasts. He socks my arms, kicks my thighs, pounds my head with his clenched fists. Red faced raging bull. Nostrils flared. Chest heaving. Eyes wide and bulging.

"Stop it, Anthony. You'll kill her!" My mother claws pitifully at my father. He's wild. Out of control. Mr. Moderation has gone bananas. Now my crazy mother is the rational one.

"Stop it, Anthony! The neighbors will hear you! Mr. Porst will call the police! Stop it!"

I'm down on the floor, struggling to protect my face and my breasts. My arms, my legs, the back of my head take the beating. I want to hit back but he scares me. His strength overwhelms me. I break down and cry. The brazen rebel has been reduced to tears. The loudmouth is scrunched into a frightened ball, a fetus, an infant crying on the floor.

The pace of the punches slows. My father stands over me, panting. He punches again. One last punch, one last kick. My mother takes his arm and tries to lead him away. He shrugs her off, walks away alone.

Before I stumble up the stairs, I see my sister standing next to my mother. She has a smirk on her face. I know that self-satisfied smirk. She enjoyed the beating. I hate her, too. I hate my father and I hate my sister.

I swear to myself, if he comes after me again I'll go straight out the front door and away from here forever.

Lee

"He must be adopted" was my mother's theory since he had that Anglo-Saxon last name and lived in a big white Protestant house on the north side of the Jersey Central railroad tracks that ran a straight line through the middle of Westfield.

He was dark. So dark my mother was sure he must be Hispanic – Puerto Rican like her, maybe. Not that being Puerto Rican was a good thing in my mother's eyes. Even though she was born in Puerto Rico, she was quick to add that her forefathers had come from Spain.

Leland Charles Beck. He was named after his father. When I first met him at a party in Bev Jones's basement, he had just returned to the States from living in England. He was wearing one of those team jackets, not silky but woolen, navy blue with BARLOW, the name of the prep school he'd attended, stitched in white felt letters on the back.

His father was an engineer. Most of the fathers in Westfield were engineers. Lee's mother was a musician, an accomplished pianist, as they say to distinguish someone like her from someone like me who could bang out a couple of tunes – a sonata here, an etude there.

Lee was thin and serious with tousled hair. Curly hair. His curls looked as if someone with long painted nails had run her fingers through them. They had a free, wild look, those curls.

And a sensuous mouth. Maybe that's what made him such a good kisser – those soft, cushiony lips. When you pressed against them, they had just the right give and just the right resistance – not too firm, not too flaccid. The give of his lips was like that one in a million pillow you're tempted to take with you when you go on vacation.

Lee was a great kisser. Not only in my book, but in Rhonda Tiger's book, too. Rhonda had been his girlfriend before me. I remember her telling me, "Lee loves to kiss." And after Lee and Rhonda broke up, I decided to find out for myself.

I had gone to a high school dance with a couple of friends. Lee was playing drums with the band. Unlike the other musicians who were laughing and goofing around on stage, Lee hardly looked up from his sparkly, maroon drum set.

So serious, I thought. And so handsome.

Toward the end of the first set, the lead singer introduced the members of the band and they each played a solo. First the lead guitarist, then the bass player, then the guy who played the sax, and then…

"Ladies and gentlemen, Lee Beck on drums!"

His drum sticks flying, Lee broke into a syncopated riff. Jazzy. A far cry from the primitive rock and roll we high school kids listened to. Soon the crowd started to lose interest. They wandered away from the stage, talking loudly among themselves. Only a few people clapped when the drum solo ended. I was one of them.

During the break, Lee sat on the sidelines. Alone. Surprised by my own boldness, I sat down beside him. I couldn't help it, he looked so forlorn. I reached out and touched his hand.

"I think your solo was great," I said. He looked at me and smiled. I never was sure who leaned towards who first. But somehow or other, our mouths connected. His lips were as soft and cool as a flower petal.

I held his long-fingered musician's hands, examined them, stroked them. I was too shy to look into his eyes.

He Hardly Ever Called

He didn't call me the way I thought a boyfriend should call his girlfriend. He'd call to find out if he could see me. We never had those long nightly, pointless conversations that my older sister had with her boyfriend. Maybe that was because Lee was too busy studying music in Manhattan, but I don't think so.

I don't think so now, but what about then? What did I think? Even then I knew he wasn't acting like a guy who was truly captivated. He was acting like a guy who could take it or leave it. Yes, I knew it, but I thought I could change his mind.

I tried to be available whenever he called to ask me out. Once when I already had said yes to a babysitting job, had given up thinking I might hear from him, he called at the last minute, on Friday night, saying he'd just arrived home for the weekend and could we get together tomorrow night.

"Oh, gee," I said, disappointed. "I can't. I'm babysitting."

"Babysitting?" Lee said. I could tell the wheels were spinning. "I can come by after the kids are asleep. You can call and let me know when."

Damn, this was dangerous. I was babysitting across the street and down the block from our house where my parents would be sitting watching TV. And what if one of the kids woke up? They'd surely tell their parents. I couldn't safely swear them to secrecy. You know how kids are. They'd say, "Yes, I swear" and then spill the beans first thing in the morning.

Mommy, guess who Annabelle had over last night – her boyfriend! And guess what they were doing?

Or what if the parents came home early and found Lee there?

"Okay, sure," I told Lee without skipping a beat.

He came over once the kids were asleep. He hadn't wanted to just sit on the sofa kissing, which was what I had in mind. Sitting close, kissing his soft lips, running my tongue across the coolness of his teeth.

He'd close his eyes and gave himself over completely to a kiss. I couldn't break away. He was too delicious, too insistent, too overwhelming. When he kissed me, my arms couldn't push away. Some drug flowed from his mouth to mine, making me incapable of saying no.

He kept touching me, kissing me as he moved me toward the stairs. Had he stopped, my mind would have cleared enough to know this was wrong, this was bad, this could lead to trouble. But, Lee kept kissing me, kept holding me as we ascended the stairs and made our way to the master bedroom.

That night for the first time he took my sweater off. For the first time I felt a man's bare chest against my breasts. For the first time, I heard myself groan. I was embarrassed. The sound was so intimate, so strange. Yet it came from me. Lee said, "It feels good, doesn't it?"

His voice broke the spell. I pushed him away and reached for my sweater, "Yes, but we'd better stop. The kids might hear us." We got up.

Lee left before the parents came home. I straightened up the covers on the bed. No one ever found out.

Rhonda Tiger

It sometimes bothered me that Lee had been seeing Rhonda Tiger before he starting going out with me. I'd seen them making out at a party. They were lying together on the couch in a friend's basement. Although fully clothed, Rhonda had her legs open wide and wrapped around Lee.

It was shocking, really, but typical of Rhonda. She was a slut. Her dyed black hair hung over one side of her face. Her teeth were crooked and it always seemed to me that if you looked you'd see food stuck between them. White bready stuff mostly, but sometimes green leafy stuff.

Do You Love Me?

Lee had given me a copy of Hemingway's For Whom the Bell Tolls. He knew I was studying Spanish history; that my high school Spanish teacher had us reading about the horrors of the bloody civil war.

Lee wanted me to read the part about sex in the sleeping bag when Rabbit feels the earth move. He wanted me to think of sex as something good. Something that would make us both feel good. He didn't understand that it also made me feel bad. Not the kissing. The kissing was guilt-free. The kissing didn't violate my sense of right and wrong. But when Lee tried to take my clothes off or touched between my legs, voices yelled inside me telling me I was bad and dirty.

I wanted Lee to love me. I wanted him to kiss me, to keep kissing me forever. I couldn't get enough. But he wanted to forge ahead.

I said, "Do you love me?"

He said, "Let me love you."

Did he mean that if I let him love me, he would *love* me?

Navy Blue Skirt

I am wearing a navy blue skirt and a navy blue sweater. They don't quite match but they're the best I have. I settle myself next to Lee in his maroon Chevy. He's been looking at my legs. Somewhere inside me I hear my mother's voice. I pull down the skirt.

Last night Lee had called to ask if I wanted to go to a concert at Juilliard – Verdi's Requiem. Oh yes, I love music. I am glad Lee is taking me out somewhere, that we are not just going to sit in his car and make out.If a boy really respects you, first you're supposed to go to a movie, go bowling, or go to a party. Then, after that, you sit in a car and kiss. If all you ever do is make out, he thinks you're cheap.

I sneak looks at Lee as he drives. His wavy black hair. His full soft lips. His intense dark eyes. His smooth, flawless skin. His hands on the steering wheel. So soft and sensitive. Such pleasure when they touch me.

We drive through the tunnel that leads to another world. We leave New Jersey and the insularity of the suburbs, the tedium of middle- class towns. We're in the big city now. We're free, sophisticated. We're artists, musicians.

We arrive too late to get seats. We stand in the back of the concert hall and I am engulfed by the music. I am lifted to the heavens. Tears fill my eyes and I believe I feel the presence of God. Lee moves closer behind me. He leans his body against mine. I am distracted from the beauty of the music. He whispers, "Let's go."

We leave the concert. We go to the room where he lives while he studies at Juilliard. The room is small and dark. The building is old and smells like the building where my Uncle Dominic lives. The acrid smell of urine, the suffocating smell of stale cigar smoke fills my nostrils. The stairs are short like Uncle Dominic's stairs. Are they marble? Some kind of stone. Whoever made them made the risers too short. Maybe when they were built, people were smaller, had smaller feet, shorter legs.

Lee and I climb those short, hard stairs to his room. A lumpy twin bed takes up most of the space. An old wooden chair stands stiff-backed beside the bed. Lee walks past the bed to the dresser. I stay standing by the door, not knowing what to do, queasy from the smell, depressed by the sight of the cracked, yellowed linoleum on the floor – the smallness, the meanness, the darkness of the room.

Lee opens the top dresser drawer. He takes out a bottle of Old Grand Dad. "Want some?" he asks. I shake my head no. He lifts a shot glass from the drawer, pours a shot from the bottle and belts it down. Is he bracing himself? For what?

He walks up to me, puts his arms around me, kisses me. His kisses aren't working as well as they usually work. The musky smell of the old linoleum, the bitter taste of the whiskey on his lips, the dinginess of the room dilute their magic. He moves me to the bed. I try to concentrate on his kisses. I try to concentrate on his soft lips, the tingling of his tongue touching the roof of my mouth, the warmth of his hands.

It almost works but he's moving too fast, holding me too tightly, kissing me too hard. He's pushing my legs apart with his knee. He's trying to take my skirt off but I won't let him. My skirt is bunched up around my waist. I won't let him take my underpants off. I won't let him. He's pushing my underpants to the side. He's pushing them aside and pushing inside me. Now he's hurting me. It's hurting. I feel as if he is trying to break me apart. He has found a vulnerable spot, a spot that can be broken, a spot that hurts when he pushes against it. If he pushed against any other part of my body it wouldn't hurt like this, but here, here between my legs it hurts. Oh, it hurts.

"It hurts," I say. "Stop, it hurts," I cry. It hurts, it burns, the pain is searing, the pain is all encompassing. I can only feel pain.

Suddenly it is over. I lie confused, not believing what just happened. I lie there and I am nothing. I think nothing. I smell nothing. I see nothing.

Lee shakes me and tells me it's late, we have to go. I push my skirt down. I pull my stockings up. I rise from the bed, walk through the door, down the hard stairs, into the maroon car.

I feel liquid ooze from between my legs. What is this? Is this what they call "come"? Am I coming? Now? Now, after it's all over, I'm coming? I don't know. I say, "I'm dripping." Lee looks at me but says nothing.

It isn't until later when I undress up in my bedroom that I find the blood soaking my underpants and stockings, staining my navy blue skirt.

See You at C.U.

It had been my father's desire that I go to Catholic University, that I spend four years enrolled there, a Catholic coed. And although I had applied to other schools and been accepted, he made it clear it would be Catholic University or no university for me.

"See you at C.U." The letter of acceptance ended on a cute note. And they did see me. My family and I – most of us, not my older sister but everyone else – my father, mother and younger sister took a trip to Washington DC to meet with the admissions people and tour the campus. It was April and I was pregnant, but I didn't know it yet.

It was during the moody month of March, the deep, unfathomable month of March when I had gone with Lee to his rented room near Juilliard, and it had happened. But I didn't have a clue when we went to visit the Catholic University campus, not even morning sickness.

It was not me but Sally, my younger sister, who threw up there on the lawn just outside the admissions office. She'd had too much soda. Her vomit was orange. She'd been allowed to have orange soda in the car to pacify her. My parents gave into her much more than they ever gave into me. Her whining brought her junk food and soda while mine brought only slaps.

The trip had been long and nauseating. My father, true to his personal code, avoided all toll roads, so it was stop and go all the way, all five or six hours. Stop and go for the four of us. Stop and go for the fetus sleeping inside me. Rockabye baby.

Sally threw up loud and hard right there on the lawn just outside the windows of the admissions office. Had the admissions counselor caught the act? We filed inside after my mother wiped the orange residue off Sally's chin, tried to straighten up her hair. We all sat down in the office of the admissions counselor assigned to us – a woman (it couldn't have been a very well paying job if they had given it to a woman, or maybe she was a nun, a plain clothes nun and this was her service to the church – greeting prospective students and their families, arranging a little tour of the campus for them.)

She saw my legs as soon as I sat down in the chair next to her desk. I could tell. Even though she masked her curiosity like a pro, I could tell she would have liked to read the blue writing on my calves. Last night, Sally had taken one of her blue magic markers and had written "You're a jerk" on my leg. I thought it was funny, so I grabbed the marker from her and wrote "Takes one to know one" on my other leg.

Big blue letters on both legs. I figured I could scrub it off, but not this ink. This was long-lasting ink, indelible. It would have to wear off gradually. Soap and water only gave the ink a slightly lighter, smudgy look. My legs still carried their message, loud and clear for the world to see – if I wore a skirt. And a skirt was what I had to wear to Catholic University, a skirt and sheer stockings. A good girl – a normal, middle class Catholic girl – did not wear opaque stockings in those days. And no pants. Not to school, not to church, and certainly not on a tour for a prospective student of Catholic University.

That morning when we were rushing around, getting ready for our trip, my parents were so engrossed in their bickering, they had not thought to make a proper inspection of their college-bound daughter.

"Aida," my father had bellowed to my mother from the living room. "It's eight o'clock already, would you get a move on, for God's sake?"

"Ai, bendito, Antoni!" my mother had yelled back from the bedroom. "I'll be there in a minute. We have plenty of time. Just hold your horses!"

I had managed to scurry off to the car before either one could take a good look at me. And once in the car, I wrapped myself in a blanket. It was April and mornings were chilly.

We arrived on time for the interview.

The admission counselor kept her gaze at eye level but I could tell she was fighting an urge to look down at my legs. "Half our student body belong to a religious order," she announced in a perky voice.

Oh, great, I thought. How could one even begin to compete for grades with priests and nuns? Study and pray was all they did. They didn't waste time dancing or dating or writing in a diary or rolling their hair in curlers or shaving their legs. They probably aced all the tests and got straight A's. They would make it impossible for a normal person to look good. Why even bother? I hadn't even enrolled yet, but already I was discouraged.

In order to decipher the writing on my calves, the admissions counselor would have to tilt her head sideways till it almost rested on her shoulder. But she wasn't going to succumb to that temptation, not with the four of us sitting there watching her. She did most of the talking – about Catholic University, about life on campus. No, she'd wait for the tour guide to arrive, the upper level student who would show us around. At some point during the distraction of introducing our guide, she'd sneak a peek.

"… and this is Annabelle. She just might be joining us here at CU next fall. She hails from Westfield, New Jersey…"

Dr. Tyndall

My mother stopped having sex with my father after she found out I was pregnant. She told me this when I was just a couple of months along, I suppose to make me feel even guiltier than I already did. Somehow it made sense to her. It never made sense to me. I knew she was punishing him, but for what? She was always punishing him. He was always punishing her. Who started it? According to her, it was he, Antoni, who started the punishment with his cheapness and his inability to show her affection.

He gave her a monthly household allowance, just barely enough to cover the cost of food for the five of us. And each month he gave her the money later than the month before so that over a year, say, or eighteen months, he saved himself a month's allowance.

Unlike my two sisters, I always sided with my mother. She was the underdog and I felt protective of her. As I was growing up she told me stories of how, when they were first married and she would reach out to take his hand as they were boarding a train or walking down a crowded city street, he'd snap his hand away. "No public displays of affection," he reminded her. No affection, public or private, it seemed to me. I never saw them kiss. Not even a little good-bye peck on the cheek. Not even a hug.

But this time – the time of my unwed pregnancy – *she* was punishing *him* for not being a better father, for allowing the unthinkable to happen.

And she punished God. She stopped going to church.

My mother and I were in the office of Dr. Tyndall when we found out why I was throwing up all the time. Dr. Violet Tyndall. My mother would only allow a woman to examine me. Had she noticed how big and square and mannish Dr. Tyndall was?

I'd been feeling sick, nauseous. All the time it seemed. Could it be one of those stomach viruses? Or nerves? It could be nerves. The doctor had given me vile green medicine to swallow. But it wasn't working. I still felt sick. The doctor decided to run some tests. When the results came back from the lab, she called us in to her office.

"You're daughter is pregnant," Dr. Tyndall said. Clutching her chest, my mother sprang up from the naugahyde chair and let out a cry. "Ai, Dios mio!" Then her knees buckled and she collapsed in a heap on the carpet.

I sat immobile, watching Dr. Tyndall struggle to help my mother up from the floor and back in her chair, my mother struggle to get her skirt back down over her knees. The garters on her girdle were showing. Lucky thing there were only us women in the room, me and the good Doctor Tyndall.

Before we left her office, Dr. Tyndall asked me if I had gone to church to confess the sin that had made me pregnant, to pray for absolution for the mortal sin I had committed.

Can you even get absolution for a mortal sin? I asked myself in the car on the way back home. Aren't mortal sins just that – mortal, irreversible, fatal?

My musings were cut short when I glanced over at my mother and saw the mortal grip she had on the steering wheel, the crazed look on her face. She was speeding through town, telling me she'd kill us both. Both? No, now there were three of us. She'd kill the three of us.

My mother learned to drive at age thirty-five and had been a timid driver ever since. She was petite – short, really, not even five feet tall – and had to crane her neck to see over the steering wheel. Her right foot shifted constantly back and forth from the gas pedal to the brake as she drove. She rarely ever reached the posted speed limit, much less exceed it.

To see her wild behind the wheel, forcing the pedal down to the car floor with all the might she had in her short, chubby right leg should have struck me as funny. But I wasn't laughing. I was hunched in my seat, afraid.

Bitter Forfeit

I can't hear Lee's voice in my mind anymore but I know it wasn't an unpleasant voice – an unusually high voice, for instance, or a scratchy voice, or one of those voices that come from a place way down in the throat, so far down that it sounds more like a machine than a human. I know I'd remember if he had a voice like that.

I can't remember much of what he said to me either, probably because he didn't say much. I hardly knew him. But I know that he wanted me to give the baby up for adoption.

I told him I had borrowed a book from the library. A book called "Bitter Forfeit." A novel about a young, unmarried woman who gets pregnant, has a baby in a home for unwed mothers and when the baby is born, gives it up, leaving it in the arms of the people who run the home. She leaves it to them to find a childless couple to be the baby's mother and father. She returns to her home and gets on with her life – her studies, her job, her circle of friends – but finds that she cannot stop wondering about the baby, has second thoughts about her decision to give it up; the decision she had been so sure was the right one, the most practical, reasonable one. But the papers she signed are final, binding. She has no rights to the child, has no right to know where the child lives or even her name. The child is a girl – that is all she knows.

A bitter forfeit. I told Lee I was not giving up my child.

"A bitter forfeit," he repeated. "Oh, if you keep this baby, it will be a bitter forfeit, that's for sure." He was letting me know that if I kept the baby, he would no longer see me. I had a choice of forfeits.

He had been somewhat sympathetic toward me before, agreeing that this was our problem to figure out together. It was only fair that we should share the responsibility for resolving it. But, now that it was not resolving itself in the direction he and his parents had envisioned, his attitude grew hostile.

Somehow we had skipped right past marriage. Without my even knowing why or being asked for my opinion on the subject, marriage had quickly been eliminated from the list of possible resolutions.

There would be no marriage. But neither would there be a bitter forfeit. There would be no giving up of the baby.

Catholic Charities

My mother and father took me to be interviewed by a woman who worked for Catholic Charities. The point of the interview, as I understood it, was to evaluate me for placement in a home for unwed mothers where I would spend the long days of my advanced pregnancy in the company of other pregnant girls under the strict supervision of – who knows, probably nuns, if not nuns, then Catholic women who acted like nuns, who might as well be nuns.

"You're a beautiful girl," the interviewer said. "You will have a beautiful baby. What does the father look like?"

I thought quickly, "Oh, he's short and fat, has freckles and bucked teeth." Maybe she'd reject me if I was going to have a funny-looking baby.

I wonder if she believed me. I wonder what she was writing down on that interview report.

Funny looking father, perhaps.

Or was it, Mother makes up stories.

Or more like, "Not straightforward with her answers."

She described the unwed mother program, "After you give birth, you will return home to your family and the baby will be adopted by a loving Catholic couple."

"Oh no," I said. "I won't give up my baby. I will keep my baby."

"Well then, you cannot stay in our home for unwed moms," she said. "You might influence our other girls to keep their babies."

That was that for Catholic Charities. In silence, we drove back to our home in Westfield. Me, sitting up tall in the middle of the back seat, feeling like a freak, my miserable, worried parents in front. Silent. The eerie silence that comes before the storm.

Just about that time, my father developed a tic in his right eye.

Tuna Casserole

I was sitting at the table in the yellow kitchen in Westfield, eating my mother's tuna casserole, a pregnant teenager, flanked by her mother and father. Sally, my younger sister sat opposite, making faces at me when our parents weren't looking.

My older sister, Ines, was away at school and I was missing her. She had been my ally, my confidante. If she had been there for me then when I really needed her, I might not have felt so completely alone. But Ines had gotten out. When she left my parents' home, she left me as well. I knew she was never coming back.

Curling back my upper lip ever so subtly, I shot Sally my gaze of poison.

"She's looking at me," Sally whined to my father in a singsong voice.

"Would you stop looking at her?" my father snapped at me. "Look at her one more time and you'll really get it." I knew when to quit. I lowered my eyes from the smirk on my sister's face and redirected them to the creamy noodles on my plate – the pink bits of tuna, the wrinkled peas.

Pregnancy was making me eat more, love food more. I particularly loved my mother's tuna casserole. I loved tuna. My mother used to say that she, herself, craved tuna when she was pregnant with me, although she never really liked tuna that much before. Or after.

I reached for the casserole dish and was helping

myself to a second serving when my mother said, "Better watch it, you're getting fat."

A Bathing Suit with a Skirt

Once, before I was sent to live at the Boraks and before I went to the Jersey shore with my girlfriends, I called Lee. My parents were tormenting me. Scorn from my father, pushing and punching from my mother.

"I have to get out for a while. I have to talk to you," I said to Lee.

He drove over to our less prosperous side of town in his maroon Chevy. I stood on the sidewalk in front of our house waiting for him so he wouldn't have to come to the door and be subjected to the craziness going on in there.

We drove to Tamaquas Park and sat in the car. I was holding his hand, stroking the softness. I told him I was going to the Jersey shore with my girlfriends.

"You should wear one of those bathing suits with a skirt," he suggested.

At first I didn't understand. I said, "You like those bathing suits with skirts?"

"To hide the pregnancy, I mean."

I wanted him to kiss me. I wanted him to touch me. I didn't even care if he – if we "went all the way." Actually, I sort of wanted to, now that there wasn't anything to lose – or gain, like a baby. I was curious to see if maybe it would feel good.

We'd only done it twice. Once that first time in Lee's rented room near Juilliard and the second time in the back seat of his car, the same car we were sitting in now. Both times I'd resisted and it hurt. Maybe this time it would feel better, feel good. Maybe it would feel so good Lee would decide he loved me, maybe he'd decide to marry me.

But Lee said, "No, we can't. You're pregnant."

We were in the car in Tamaquas Park just that one time. There would be other times when I'd call him in desperation, but never again would he come to me.

A Craving for Liverwurst

I was at the Jersey shore with a group of girlfriends. I was still a reasonable size, a normal teenage-girl-size, and my friends didn't know, or at least I didn't think they knew. I hadn't told them.

We were staying in the house of the grandmother of one of my friends. I brought my liverwurst with me, a big roll of it. I was craving liverwurst, or maybe it was the baby craving liverwurst. Either way, I needed liverwurst. And to ensure I'd have enough of it while I was at the shore, I brought a thick log of it with me. My mother must have bought it. I didn't have my own money. Any money I earned from babysitting went straight to my mother and was put in the bank.

I stored the liverwurst in the refrigerator and snacked on it when the cravings called me so loudly I couldn't ignore them. I'd make a sandwich, so I wouldn't seem too weird. I'd take the time to unwrap the liverwurst, slice off a quarter inch or so and tuck it between two slices of bread, one painted with mustard, the other plain. I'd even take the time to cut the sandwich in half before biting into it. My restraint was all a show for my friends and the grandmother. Had they not been around, I'd have clutched the liverwurst with both hands and gnawed right into it.

Bubbles in My Belly

The baby was blowing bubbles inside me. That's what it felt like sometimes. The first time I felt him blowing bubbles I was back home from my week at the Jersey shore, hiding in my room, steering clear of my mother and her rampages.

Laughter, I thought. The baby is laughing, chuckling. Hey, what's so funny, baby? Nobody else thinks it's so funny. Nobody else seems able to find any humor in this situation.

My mother is angry, "How could you do this to me?" she screams. "How could God allow this to happen?"

My father is trying to figure out what to do. His brow furrows as he considers, "What's the best way to handle this situation, the best way for the family? Should the child be put up for adoption?"

My father the strategist, the activist, assessed the situation, came up with a game plan and took action as my mother wept and chased me around the house.

"You're a disgrace. Look at you with that big belly. You were once a beautiful rosebud. Now you're faded, used, discarded. Who will ever want you now? What man will ever marry you now? Your life is ruined!"

We were at the top of the stairs. A minute before she had come crashing through the door of my room, slamming it back against the wall, lunging at me, punching me, slapping me. I made for the stairs. If I could get down the stairs and out the door, into the open, I could out-run her, escape her flailing arms, her screams, her insults.

"I'll push you down the stairs" she yelled, coming at me with both arms outstretched like a zombie. But I held on to the banister. I clung to it as she pushed against me.

She wasn't as big, as strong, as young, as I was. She couldn't budge me. She broke down and cried. She dropped her hands in defeat, in despair. She turned away from me, sobbing.

Should I console her? Should I touch her shoulder? Should I say softly, Mom, please don't cry. I'm sorry, Mommy. I'm sorry I hurt you. Please, please don't cry.

Pills for Depression

My father decided to take me to see a psychiatrist who prescribed pills for depression when I told him I had no energy, I slept most of the day. I never knew what kind of pills they were. I only knew they were supposed to make me feel better, happier. Were they supposed to make me more compliant, more agreeable to giving up my baby? Were they supposed to make me see the wisdom in giving up the baby? Were they supposed to make me so blissful, so euphoric that I wouldn't care if my baby were taken from me?

I only took the pills once. Within a half-hour of swallowing them, I wound up on the floor, squeezing my breasts together with my arms to stop the pounding pain. It was as if something were growing inside my breasts, growing bigger than the skin could tolerate, growing and pushing against blood vessels.

I groaned and rocked side to side, hugging my chest. Seeing me there on the bedroom floor, my mother, who guarded and dispensed the pills, vowed to throw the remainder down the toilet and be done with them. She had my father call the psychiatrist and explain why we were stopping the pills.

There were no more pills after that. The psychiatrist didn't prescribe another type, another brand. We just dropped the idea.

The Psychiatrist

His last name was Irish – a one syllable, Irish last name. Hayes? Boyle? Doyle? Yes, Doyle. Maybe my father hoped Dr. Doyle would be able to talk some sense into me, convince me of the wisdom in giving up my child. As it was, things at home were becoming unbearable for him. Just the sight of her pregnant daughter was driving my mother to alternate between violent attacks and extended periods, sprawled fully-clothed in bed, hiding her face under a pillow.

Oh, you couldn't actually tell yet. Annabelle just looked a little more filled-out. But soon, very soon the pregnancy would be impossible to disguise. What to do with her, where to send her? Time was running out.

The psychiatrist worked with my father to find a place for me, away from friends, neighbors, those who knew me, knew the family. The tall, thin, creepy psychiatrist. I see him sitting with his skinny legs closely entwined. I see him with his clenched hands resting on his boney knee. Even through his pants you could tell his knees were boney.

He had four young children, this psychiatrist, and one day he invited me to go to the movies with him and his kids. We sat through an afternoon of Jerry Lewis movies, a special matinee.

I think there may have been a plan afoot for me to go live with the psychiatrist and be his babysitter. The matinee may have been a testing ground for that plan. But it was soon dropped. Who knows why. Maybe I ate too much popcorn. Maybe the psychiatrist's wife said no. Maybe my father nixed the plan. At any rate, an alternative scheme was formulated: I would be sent to live with the Boraks – a family Dr. Doyle had worked with recently.

The Boraks

I was sent to live with the Boraks so that the neighbors and my younger sister would not know that I was pregnant. The story was that I was away in college, Catholic University in Washington DC. But I was really in Watchung, New Jersey, at the Boraks.

Mrs. Borak must have felt that she, too, had to make up a story about me. She told her friends that I was a relative from Wisconsin who had come to stay with her for a while. Wisconsin? Where's that?

My baby would be born on November 25. I went to live with the Boraks at the end of August, just when the new school year was about to start, before my pregnant condition became obvious.

The Borak family – a husband, wife and two daughters – lived in Watchung in a red brick house. It seems odd to list the husband first. In the Borak family, father came last. The father was a stocky shadow figure who was rarely home. And when he was home, no one paid any attention to him. I think he was embarrassed to have a pregnant teenager living in his house. I never really got a sense of who he was. (Well, no. That's wrong. I did get a sense. A blue collar worker, construction maybe, garbage man perhaps.) He left for work early each morning in his dark blue work clothes, carrying his lunch pail. A big one. It had to be extra big, for he had a big appetite. He ate big sandwiches. Whatever he ate, he ate in a sandwich, including chicken legs, bone-in. I never saw him eat a chicken leg sandwich – but Mrs. Borak told me that he did. I imagined it was a messy business.

No chicken for Giggles, however, the younger of their two daughters (but not as young as you'd think from her nickname). She'd been given that name when she was a baby in a highchair. She loved to be tickled and would giggle uncontrollably when her mother, palms outstretched and fingers writhing would tease, "Here I come, little Giggles. I'm coming to tickle your belly!"

Now, at sixteen, the unfortunate nickname had stuck.

No chicken for Giggles for she was a vegetarian. She didn't want an animal to be killed for her. She told me that since she became a vegetarian, her belly had grown more prominent. "What's really weird is I haven't gained weight." She said. "It's just that my belly pops out more now."

"Vegetables and lentils take up more room than meat, you know," she theorized, "and you have to eat more of them to feel full."

I'd been thinking about becoming a vegetarian. It seemed a noble thing to do. How could I profess to love animals and then sit down at the dinner table to devour a lamb, a piglet, a calf?

But this new information about a pot belly caused me to reconsider.

"Gee," I thought out loud. "Maybe vegetarianism isn't such a good idea after all. A round belly? Not for me." Since sixth grade, I had prided myself on my flat abdomen.

"Well, having a baby is gonna make your tummy fat, anyway. Look at my mother. Look at your mother. All women who've had babies have pot bellies!"

Giggles

Giggles and I played Monopoly together, we took walks in the woods near her house, we painted each other's toenails *Love That Pink* and shared secrets. Her friendship helped to fill the void left by my older sister who had gone off to nursing school. Never wrote. Never called. Had she been infected by the scorn my parents felt for me? Maybe she feared that if she were too sympathetic, my parents would suspect that she might be having sex with her boyfriend down there at school and would insist that she come home.

Giggles and I had a lot in common. We both loved animals and we'd gone to the same psychiatrist. I was still going; she had stopped. She had been sent to the psychiatrist after a suicide attempt.

She told me that it was her mother's idea to send her to the psychiatrist. Her father didn't believe in psychiatry. His answer to all of life's setbacks was ice cream. Many a time when she was a little girl and came home from school in tears because some bully had pushed her or made fun of her, Mr. Borak would drive her over to the nearest Stewarts and order them each a triple scoop cherry vanilla ice cream sundae drizzled with chocolate syrup, topped with whipped cream and a maraschino cherry. He never understood what a psychiatrist could do that a generous serving of ice cream couldn't do better.

The Sculptor

Giggles told me about her experiences with the psychiatrist, Dr. Doyle who fancied himself a sculptor. What did he sculpt? Stone? Did he chisel stone? I pictured him molding shapes from clay, a huge mound of dung-colored plasticene piled on a flat disk, a lazy Susan-type contraption that spins this way or that so you don't have to walk around your work as you mold it, pat it, dig at it, press it.

Giggles told me she posed for the psychiatrist. He said it was part of her therapy. She told me Dr. Doyle asked her to take off her clothes. And she did. All of them? I wondered, but was too shy to ask. I wanted it to be just her shirt. I didn't want to think of her sitting there completely naked, vulnerable. Sixteen years old. A year younger than me. That past winter, despondent over all the starving deer in the woods behind her house, she had tried to kill herself by swallowing a bottle of tranquilizers.

Giggles was too sensitive for this world. Too tenderhearted.

She told me the psychiatrist took his pants off as he worked on the clay figure he was forming on the swivel disk. Did he say he was getting hot? Did he say he could work more comfortably with no pants on? He needed to work unencumbered? He felt restricted in pants, and in order to create art, he needed to take his pants off?

As Giggles related her story, I pictured Dr. Doyle in baggy, striped undershorts and long black hose reaching up to his boney knees. The image made me shiver with disgust.

Is This Therapy?

I was sitting in the chair in his office, answering his questions as best I could. The whole thing made me nervous; sitting there being scrutinized by this weird man, this man who thought he knew everything, whose attitude toward me was patronizing. Just this side of scornful.

He seemed to only want to talk about sex. He wanted me to tell him all the details. I didn't, of course. I said something vague – not purposely vague for I was so naïve, so overwhelmed, so puzzled by all that was happening to me, I didn't have the wherewithal to be illusive.

I had no women's wiles. I never learned to be manipulative or cagey. Maybe I was too dumb, too stupid. But when I answered his questions, I was answering as honestly as I could, considering how difficult it was for me to talk to him, to relate to him, this weird old man. I said something about not meaning to, not wanting to do it – the penetration thing. I only wanted the kissing. I didn't want that final disgusting hurtful thing – that embarrassing act. Even the word "act" sounded embarrassing.

Dr. Doyle responded in a condescending tone, "Oh, come now,'" he began. "Don't tell me you didn't enjoy it."

"I enjoyed some of it." I already told you that, you weirdo, I thought to myself.

"I see, and what part of it did you enjoy?" he pursued, lowering his voice to feign intimacy.

Was this therapy? Was this going to solve the problem of my pregnancy? Was this going to cure me of whatever condition I had?

I Couldn't Say No

In the straight-backed chair Dr. Doyle had planted in the center of his office, I squirmed, twisting a strand of my dark brown hair round and round my finger, darting my eyes to avoid his probing gaze. He sat motionless, sculpture-like in his padded recliner. It seemed we would sit like that forever, but then without a word he pushed against the arms of the recliner raising himself up and walked towards me. For a long, silent moment, he tapped his chin with the index finger of his right hand, circling my chair like a coyote stalking a stray lamb.

He was embarrassing me, ogling me, murmuring, "Hum, beautiful. Beautiful lines. You know, I'd like to sculpt you."

"Oh," I said.

I couldn't say no. Though I wanted to, I couldn't. I didn't know how to say no to anyone except my mother, my sisters, and sometimes to my father, when I was feeling brave. "Fresh" was the word my parents used. Not brave, but fresh. Yet I wasn't feeling fresh or brave under Dr. Doyle's close scrutiny. I felt like running away.

Later, in the car with my father on the way back to the Boraks, I sat with my eyes shut tight , my hands clenched, screwing up the courage to tell my father what I knew about

Dr. Doyle. It meant talking about sex. To my father. But I had to do it. It was that or return to the boney lecher.

"Dad, Giggles told me Dr. Doyle made her take her clothes off and pose for him. And while she was posing, he took his pants off in front of her!" I blurted out. I had to force it out or it would have stayed stuck inside me, festering.

"I can't go back to him, Dad. Please don't make me go back. He gives me the creeps!" I waived my hands furiously to ward off the specter of Dr. Doyle in his boxer shorts. I covered my face in my hands waiting for my father's response.

We drove in silence through the outskirts of Watchung toward the Borak's red brick raised ranch.

At last, he spoke as he parked the car alongside the row of precisely trimmed hedges that lined the front lawn. "We'll see," he said.

I could tell by his arched eyebrows that he was considering what I had just told him. I knew from the furrowed forehead that he wasn't dismissing my story as a teenage fabrication. Something in what I said or how I said it rang true to him. I could tell.

Hopeless

I don't know how much my father told Dr. Doyle. I don't know if he elaborated on why I refused to go back. But, I do know that Dr. Doyle said I was hopeless, or at least that's what my father told me.

"I asked him if I should find someone else to treat you, another psychiatrist. But he said if he couldn't help you, no one could," my father told me.

I wanted to protest, to defend myself, but I knew it was pointless. How could I, the problem child, expect to change my father's mind?

At least I don't have to go back, I thought. Better leave well enough alone.

I was hopeless. And fresh. Getting fresher and fresher. My attitude toward Mrs. Borak – silly, skinny, stupid Mrs. Borak – surpassed fresh. It was belligerent.

I Didn't Last Long at the Boraks

It couldn't have been more than a month that I spent there, holding my breath, sleeping a lot, trying to make the time go faster.

When September came and Giggles returned to High School for her senior year, I was left in the house all day long with only Mrs. Borak as a companion. I stayed in my room most of the time, reading and sleeping. I had degenerated into a moody recluse, a strange dark figure, like a vampire in her coffin, who didn't come out of her room until Giggles came home. That room was small enough to be a coffin. All that would fit was one twin bed with a nightstand squeezed against the side.

I tried to time my visits to the kitchen when Mrs. Borak was downstairs doing laundry or out shopping so I wouldn't have to see her or talk to her. But sometimes I miscalculated. Late one dreary afternoon, thinking the coast was clear, I slunk out of my room and into the kitchen heading for the refrigerator. Mrs. Borak was sitting quietly at the kitchen table, waiting for me. She told me she had called Lee's house, had spoken to his father and then to Lee. "I told Lee how pregnant you are, how unhappy you are. And then I asked him point blank, I said, 'How can you *do* this to her? What kind of a *man* are you? It's not too late, you know, to do the right thing, make an honest woman of her, marry her!'"

She told me that Mr. Beck had answered the phone. When she asked to speak to Lee, he said, "Which one? The old Lee Lee or the young Lee Lee?"

I imagined her giggling her silly giggle as she answered, "Why, the young Lee Lee, please."

That's how stupid she was. She thought Mr. Beck had said Lee Lee, when he had said Leland. I was boiling over with rage, hot faced with embarrassment.

The Hungarian Couple

Mrs. Borak must have given my father some time to devise another plan, to come up with another place for me to stay. I wondered how he found the next one, but I wouldn't ask and risk the sharp edge of his scorn. The wayward daughter had no right to ask.

Did he find the Hungarian couple through Dr. Doyle? No, the Hungarians were a stable, happily-married man and wife who once owned a bakery and were now retired and living along the Jersey shore where taxes were low. They would never be associated with a creep like him.

With their kind eyes and plump figures, the Hungarian couple reminded me of Santa and Mrs. Claus, except instead of red they wore white. White baker aprons. They collaborated in the kitchen, creating chunky goulashes, delicate pastry, aromatic stewed fruit. They were great cooks and I was an appreciative boarder. Yes, I was a boarder. Maybe they had put an ad in the Jersey shore newspaper for a boarder. Maybe that's how my father found them.

I slept in the spare bedroom on a puffy, extra high twin bed. The mattress and box spring were so thick that if I wanted to sit on the bed, I would have to rise up on my toes in order to plant my bottom squarely on the mattress. Once up there, I felt like the princess of the Princess and the Pea story – but without the pea. In this bed, all was soft and comforting. The baby and I slept long and well.

My father told the Hungarian couple that I was married to a young man who was in the Army. Overseas. He never wrote to me. During the weeks that I boarded there, no letters came. Oh, but I talked about him, my husband, my young, brave husband, the father of this baby I was carrying. At the dinner table I described for them how handsome he was, how he played the drums, some of the funny things he said.

"He's a serious musician, you know. He studied at Juilliard."

"Oh, how nice," the wife said.

"He does this hilarious imitation of a chicken," I went on. "He walks around flapping his arms, scratching the ground with his feet, poking his head forward and back. Here, I'll show you." I got up from my chair and strutted around the table, sticking my big belly out so far I nearly lost my balance.

"Be careful, sweet Anna," the wife said. "Remember you're carrying a baby." They nicknamed me "sweet Anna" after a type of paprika, Édés Anna, used in Hungarian cuisine.

Most of the houses in that town along the Jersey shore were summer homes, inhabited only during the summer months. The owners might drive down for a quiet, off-season weekend, but that late fall when I was staying with the Hungarian couple, most of the houses were quiet, closed up, waiting for their owners to return with the warm weather.

The streets were empty. Rarely did a car pass by. This stretch of Jersey shore was a long thin finger of an island. The southern tip was surrounded by sea with no bridge or ferry to take you further. Whenever I saw a car heading south, past the

Hungarian couple's house, I knew that sooner or later the car would pass again from the opposite direction.

It was a peaceful time for me and the baby. The Hungarian couple never disturbed us, never told us to get up. Never purposely made noise so we'd wake up.

I'd go for long walks along the shore – long, long walks without ever seeing another human being. Just sea gulls. I'd walk along the hard-packed, damp sand near the ocean's edge. Sometimes I'd stop and sit on the sand, gazing out to sea, without a thought.

Yellow Cottage

My father moved me a third time – from the home of the Hungarian couple along the Jersey shore to Somerville where I spent the last leg of my pregnancy in a little rented cottage. I'd been happy with the Hungarian couple. It wasn't that I'd gotten in trouble with them. They hadn't asked my father to move me out. No, this time I was being moved to be closer to Somerset Hospital where I would deliver my baby, where Tony would make his entrance, or rather his exit – his exit from me and into the world that lay outside.

Dr. Anthony Del Basso, the little Italian doctor my father had chosen, worked in Somerset Hospital.

I took long walks down the wooded road outside the yellow cottage which had a living room, a bedroom, a bathroom and a kitchen, that was about it. Oh, and a screened-in porch. The house sat at the cul-de-sac of a wooded road. The trees along the road grew denser as you drove toward the little house. For heavily-populated New Jersey with its sprawling suburbs, this road was a rarity. It was a good road to walk along.

My father had bought me a book to read, Childbirth Without Fear. As you might guess from its title, the main premise of the book was that without fear, childbirth is painless. The author (a man) considered himself an expert on the subject. He believed that only the fear in a woman's heart causes childbirth to be painful.

He suggested that walking during pregnancy helped the child bearing process. So I walked. Oh, I probably would have anyway, even if the author had said a woman should never walk during pregnancy. I liked to walk.

Along my way down the wooded road, dogs would run out from their yards to greet me. They'd drop whatever they were doing, even if it was digging a hole or sniffing a pile of rabbit droppings, to come greet the pregnant girl from the yellow cottage. I'd pet them, scratch behind their ears a bit, then continue on my way, the dogs either taking the lead or prancing by my side.

By the end of my walk, we'd be a sizeable group – one very pregnant human and six smiling canines.

In the yellow cottage, I had a clock radio that sat on the night table by my bed. I forced myself to listen to the adult stations – the Henry Mancini, Peggy Lee, Frank Sinatra stations – the "easy listening" stations. I tried to cut myself off from rock and roll. I thought you had to, a girl had to if she were going to have a baby. A mother couldn't, shouldn't listen to rock and roll.

Thanksgiving Dinner

My mother took me to a restaurant for Thanksgiving dinner, three days before the Sunday when Tony would be born.

By that time, I was puffed out like a blimp in the frilly maternity dress my mother had bought me when I could no longer fit into normal clothes – not even hers. The elastic in the lace-trimmed baby doll sleeves pinched my upper arms. The front of the dress spread out like a tent across my big belly, my protruding navel and my once-slender waist that had grown four times its former size.

My mother broke down and cried in the restaurant, sobbed over her turkey dinner, wept to see her daughter so pregnant.

"Your life is ruined," she said. "No man will have you now."

My mother stayed with me in the little cottage from Thanksgiving through the birth of my baby.

What did we do in those small rooms together? How did we spend the time? Me, reading. She, knitting, quiet now. No more histrionics. My mother was calmer now that my father had concocted a plan, laid out a strategy they could follow. Had he already decided that they would pretend to be the baby's parents? I don't think so, since we did not yet know the baby's gender. I wonder now if my father would have been so anxious to act as my baby's father if he had been a girl. Somehow I felt I'd have had a better chance fighting to keep my child if it had been a girl.

A boy was what my father had always wanted. In my father's eyes, boys were vastly superior. Every man should have a son. But he had fathered three daughters. It seemed the gods were mocking him.

He'd tell us, "I used to think that if a man had to have a daughter, his consolation would be that she would wait on him hand and foot. And if a man had three daughters, he would be like a king in his castle – but not with you girls." He'd look directly at me when he said that last part.

I should have been a boy. When my mother was carrying me, it was common knowledge that you could tell a baby's sex by the shape of the mother's belly. A belly that contained a boy child popped out. The mother looked like she'd swallowed a bowling ball. With a girl, the bulge wrapped around the mother's middle like an inner tube. My mother's protruding belly was a sure indication of a boy – a big boy.

Heart Burn

I'd only been asleep for a couple of hours that Saturday night after Thanksgiving dinner when the pains in my abdomen grew so strong I couldn't sleep.

Heart burn, I lied to myself. It couldn't be labor pains because I had already decided I wasn't going to give birth. I would just stay pregnant. Forever. Pregnancy wasn't so bad considering the alternative.

I got up to go to the bathroom, tip-toeing softly past the bed where my mother slept, a twin bed parallel to mine. Before she came to stay, I'd take turns sleeping on one bed one night and the other bed the next. I didn't want to play favorites and make one bed jealous of the other.

I purposefully didn't flush the toilet that night. I didn't want to wake my mother. I was afraid. She'd probably want to take me to the hospital and I didn't want to go.

No, if I have to have this baby, I'll have it here, I thought. Mom can boil water. Between the two of us, we'll figure it out.

I would have to be really quiet, lie still in my bed so my sleeping mother would not suspect I was having pains. It was the wee hours of the morning. There was plenty of time before dawn when she'd wake up. By then, the baby would come and there would be no need to go to the hospital.

But I couldn't keep quiet. The time came when I had no control over my groans. I tried to hold them in but they burst out of me.

"You're in labor, aren't you?"

"No, no, Ma. It's just a stomach ache."

My mother had us ready and in the car in no time. She sped through the empty, early morning streets of Somerville, ignoring stop signs and running red lights as she headed for the hospital.

Soon we were stopped by a policeman. He opened the car door on my mother's side and peered in.

"What do you think you're doing, lady …?"

"My daughter, she's having a baby, she's in labor, she …"

His gaze shifted to the figure huddled in the passenger seat, doubled over, clutching her belly, groaning loudly.

"Which hospital? Somerset? Okay, follow me." He jumped back in his black squad car, kept the siren and lights going as he escorted us to our destination.

Sunday's Child

I lay there in misery, through hours of torturous pain – grabbing on to the sides of the hospital bed. The nurses had put up railings on either side. I felt as if I were in a big white crib – a hot, bloody crib that gave no comfort.

The nurses were busy running from room to room, tending to all the other ladies giving birth that Sunday morning. They were too busy to spend time with me, to stroke my forehead, to hold my hand, to give me courage. They'd pop in for a few minutes to check on the progress of the baby's descent and to straighten out the sheets – wet with sweat and the pinkish fluid gushing out of me.

Where was my mother? Maybe the nurses decided she was in no shape to deal with the sight of her daughter in labor. Maybe they felt she would only make things worse.

I thrashed and writhed with each searing jolt of pain, the top and bottom sheets twisting around me as though I were a badly wrapped mummy. I begged for water, but was only allowed the touch of shaved ice against my lips.

"Push," one of the nurses ordered. "Hold on to the sides of the bed and push." But when I pushed, it hurt even more. As soon as the nurse left the room to check on the screamer across the hall, I stopped pushing.

After hours of writhing and screaming, the baby's head was finally there at the end of the birth canal, waiting for another strong contraction to propel it forth into the midday light streaming through the hospital window. It was then that they decided to give me a sedative.

All the hard work had been done. In minutes the baby would be born. Just before the glorious moment of birth that would have made it all worthwhile, they put me out.

"I can see your little *daughter's* head. She has dark brown hair," one of the nurses said.

Boom. Lights out.

Never dreaming the nurse might be wrong, I woke up believing I had given birth to a girl.

I'll have this one little girl and that will be that, I thought. I'll never get pregnant again. Never, ever! But even though my baby's a girl, I will love her anyway – just as much as if she were a boy.

Secretly, I had really wanted a boy. I had been influenced by my father and believed that boys had more value.

The nurse brought the baby from the nursery for me to hold, a tiny red-faced bundle in a blue blanket. Blue. The nurse had been wrong.

Anthony of Padua

Naturally, my father picked an Italian doctor – Anthony Del Basso, a nice, old school Italian who viewed my pregnancy the same way my father did, as a great shame.

When I named my baby Anthony, my father thought I had named the baby after him. Dr. Del Basso, on the other hand, assumed the baby had been named with him in mind. "Why, I'm flattered," he said when I told him the baby's name.

The truth was I had named Tony after a different Anthony – Anthony of Padua, the saint who had been watching over me since I was a little girl. St. Anthony had been my sole comfort throughout the pregnancy. He always loved me, never scorned me no matter how much trouble I was in. But I let my father and the doctor believe what they wanted. I knew St. Anthony didn't mind.

The Old School

Medical students of the old school were taught that women need plenty of bed rest after delivering a baby. True to his training, the doctor gave instructions for the nurses to keep me in bed for five days. I was not allowed to walk around like the other mothers in the room who were up and about, although a little bent over, clutching their bellies, holding them in place as if they might fall off. I had to stay in bed even though I was young and healthy.

Dr. Del Basso was short, so short I could barely see his head down there when he examined me. Yet even though I towered over him when we stood side by side, he treated me like a wayward child – but with kindness. I think he cared for me, tried his best to help me, the problem child, the one who brought untold shame upon the family.

The doctor didn't want me to nurse, neither did my mother. After all, I wasn't a *legitimate* mother. Why should I act like one? There was no husband to come get me and the baby. So why encourage me? Why encourage the fantasy of my being a real mother?

But Dr. Del Basso and my mother weren't around all that much. And when they weren't, I nursed Tony for those five days in the hospital. I nursed the little bundle, the little red-faced guy, swaddled in the blue blanket, the little baby who never wanted to leave, who stuck on, wouldn't let go when they'd try to put him back in his cart and wheel him back to the nursery. He wanted to stay lying next to me with his mouth gently resting on my nipple, so he could continue to suckle whenever he pleased. He'd drift off to a delicious nap, then his little lips would start moving again. Why take him away? Why not let him stay here in bliss?

Out of the team of nurses assigned to the maternity ward, two of them let him stay with me until the end of their shifts. Tony would cry but they had to take him back to the nursery.

I nursed Tony for five days and had no intention of stopping. Yet, when we left the hospital, my mother was carrying a supply of bottled formula ordered by doctor.

"We don't need formula, Mom. I'm nursing the baby," I said. But my mother took them with us anyway.

Pink Pills

I was holding Tony in my arms in the back seat of the car when my mother and father drove me to the yellow cottage from Somerset Hospital. My father pulled the car into the driveway. I remember that moment so clearly, the feeling of being me at that moment. Bittersweet. Sweet to have Tony in my arms, bitter because we had to return secretly to our hideout. That's what it felt like, that cottage, a den of subterfuge and deception. Like a gangster, I was holed up in a secret hideaway.

I entered the cottage, carrying my baby through the living room and went straight into the bedroom where I took off my coat, unbuttoned my blouse and nursed him.

My mother came in with a glass of water and handed me a pink pill to swallow. "Here, take this," she said. "It's a vitamin. It will keep you and the baby nice and healthy."

The next morning she gave me another pink vitamin. By the following day, my milk had dried up. No amount of sucking on Tony's part could produce more than a few trickles from my breasts. Those pink vitamins had their intended effect.

Later, when all the milk was gone, my mother confessed that the pills had been given to her by the doctor who felt that nursing would only make it harder for me to separate myself from the baby.

My poor breasts. I had felt so proud, so purposeful feeding this baby, being his source of nourishment. Now my breasts hung deflated, shrunken, grief stricken.

I wanted to strike out in rage. I wanted to rail against this violation of my right to nurse my child, my child's right to be nursed by his mother.

I wanted to smash plates. I felt like throwing the clock radio and all its easy listening music out the window.

But my baby was sleeping so I kept quiet.

Back in Westfield

Within a couple of weeks of Tony's birth, my parents decided I was ready to leave the yellow cottage, leave the baby there in Somerville with my mother, and return to Westfield. Tony had timed his birth perfectly to allow me to be home during Christmas break. So the story was told to all who might inquire that I had been away at Catholic University and was now home for the holidays.

My mother stayed an extra week in the yellow house so that her return didn't appear to be connected with mine. Friends and family were told that she'd gone to Puerto Rico to bring home the baby that she and my father would adopt, a boy child just born to a distant relative, a poor misfortunate second cousin who already had ten children and could not afford to care for another.

Don't Look at Him That Way

Time after time, I'd been warned by my father, "Don't look at him that way. Everyone will know you're his mother." By Christmas, it seemed to me my father had repeated his warning at least a thousand times – well, maybe only ninety – three times a day for each day that had passed since Tony's birth.

"Would you stop mooning at him?"

"Don't look at him with those hound dog eyes."

It was the expression on my face, in my eyes, that riled my father – a look of adoration mixed with longing.

That Christmas we shared our holiday meal with our old friends, the O'Reillys. A family just like ours – a husband, wife and three girls. My father, whose heart was not easily won, harbored a tender affection for Felix O'Reilly. Their friendship was cemented by a bond of mutual empathy. They had both lived with the heartbreak of being denied, time and time and time again, the blessing of a male child. They could feel each other's pain.

But now, for my father, at last the curse had been lifted. He proudly presented Tony as his long-desired son.

As he lined us up around the piano for a photo, he must have had to bite down hard on his tongue in order to squelch the urge to warn me again not to look at Tony *that way*, but with the O'Reillys right there in the room with us, how could he?

I still have the old photo of the group of us gathered around the piano. My mother is holding a new born in her arms. Everyone is smiling into the camera. Except for me. I'm looking at the baby.

Was I deliberately defying my father? Or, on that day of Tony's first Christmas, could I simply not help myself?

The Book Bag

When I started school at NYU a couple of months after Tony was born, my parents bought me a new suede coat. The new coat carried one stipulation: I was not to hold my school books in my arms, which was how I had carried my books in High School. "You'll wear out the suede where the books rub back and forth across your coat," my father said.

And although I didn't want one, he bought me a book bag so I could carry my books a safe distance from the new coat.

At the time I was trying to please him, trying to be the daughter he wanted me to be. Pleasing him might make him more agreeable to letting me be my son's mother, I reasoned. I put my school books in the fake leather bag even though I felt like a dork, a nerd, a Catholic school fink, walking around with the book bag at my side. It was olive green with gold-tone metal reinforcements covering the corners – like a foot locker. I lugged it on the train my father and I took from Westfield to Jersey City. I hauled it with me onto the ferry and then the subway. My father and I separated at the ferry stop in Manhattan. He walked off to Rector Street and I took the A train to West 4th.

Feeling free, I started swinging the book bag as I emerged from the subway. If I had to carry the stupid thing, at least I could have some fun with it. I swung the bag in time to the rhythm of my shoes on the concrete sidewalk, a rock 'n roll tune playing in my head.

"If you don't know how to do it, I'll show you how to walk the dog."

I entered the classroom building and jogged down the corridor to catch the elevator, my book bag swinging wildly at my side. The elevator doors opened just as the bag was arcing forward. I felt the impact of books and reinforced leather against flesh as my book bag collided with the groin of a male student rushing out of the elevator. Before I could react, the crowd behind me pushed me forward onto the elevator. Just as the doors slid shut, I caught a glimpse of a male figure doubled over, moaning.

Tons of Fun

Being at school all day long temporarily distracted me from Tony, but the weekends were unbearable. I would stay home all day, hovering around my mother as she fed him, bathed him. She wouldn't allow me to do much for him. Only as much as a sister would.

Tony slept in a crib in my parents' bedroom while I slept alone in my room upstairs. There were times when I'd scoop Tony in my arms and carry him up to my bedroom. I'd give him a tour of my room pointing out objects I thought would interest him – my old Barbie doll, a shiny rhinestone pendant. Then I'd prop him up on my bed, surround him with pillows like a little pasha, and tickle his belly.

Sooner or later, Tony would get fussy and let me know it was time for his bottle. We'd have to go downstairs. To face reality. No more pretending that we were in our own little house together with no mother and father downstairs to remind me, "You're not capable of taking care of a child. You can't even take care of yourself."

Once I was rocking Tony in the black rocker my parents kept in the TV room. The slow, gentle rocking motion that would normally lull the little guy to sleep wasn't working. His big brown eyes wouldn't close. I picked up the pace. Tony started to giggle. "Faster, faster!" he seemed to be saying, even though he couldn't talk yet.

"Well, okay, if you're not going to sleep, we may as well have some fun," I said.

Faster and faster we went – way, way forward, then way, way back. The rocker teetered, lost contact with the floor and landed on its side. Tony, safely cradled in my arms, squealed with delight.

Maybe in my parent's eyes I wasn't a good mother, but to Tony I was tons of fun.

The Newman Club

That first semester at NYU I tried as hard as I could to be what I thought was a "good girl." I attended every class, took notes at every lecture, completed every assignment. I joined the Newman Club, a club for Catholic students. I spent my free time between classes in the Newman Club lounge. I thought I'd be safe there. I figured there'd be no temptation there – no attractive boys.

Father Murphy and Father Flanagan

Father Murphy, a young Franciscan priest, was the advisor to the Catholic students. He was unlike any priest I had ever known, friendly, approachable, human.

Compared to Father Flanagan back at Holy Trinity Church in Westfield, Father Murphy was an unexpected blessing, a gift from God. To me, he embodied all the qualities of compassion and forgiveness that I associated with Christ.

Once when I was a junior in high school, Father Flanagan had substituted for our regular catechism teacher. "Sister Mary Joseph has come down with the flu, or some such malady," Father Flanagan said, not bothering to disguise his disdain for the weakness that brought on Sister's sickness, that caused her to shirk her duty to the parish – the teaching of catechism to heathen teenagers whose parents didn't have the good sense to send them to Catholic school.

"Who can recite the Apostle's Creed for me?" Father Flanagan asked, testing the waters to see just how ignorant we were. "Right now! You there in the back, close that prayer book. I'll have no cheating in this class."

My hand shot up. If there was one thing I was good at, it was memorizing prayers. I knew them all and had even won a little plastic statue of the Virgin Mary for reciting perfectly, by heart, the Acts of Faith, Love and Contrition plus the Salve Regina.

Father Flanagan ignored me, turning his round red face towards the boy's side of the classroom. And even though no boy had raised his hand, the priest called on Roland Carmagno who was sitting up in the front, looking reasonably alert.

Roland botched the prayer, but Father Flanagan didn't seem to mind. "Good try, Roland. Please return to your seat."

And so it went. Father would ask a question but never called on a girl to answer. He acted as if we weren't there.

Toward the end of the interminable hour that we were obliged to spend in that stuffy Catholic classroom, Father Flanagan gave the boys some heart to heart advice.

"Stay away from girls," he warned. "They're dirty and they'll lead you into trouble."

In God's Hands

One day when I was at school, my mother took Tony, now six months old, to the pediatrician for his DPT vaccination. Tony had a cold on the day of his appointment. My mother had called the doctor to find out whether she should keep the appointment or reschedule it for the following week.

"Bring him in," said the doctor. "We can give him his shot today. There'll be no problem."

That night after the shot, Tony's cold moved deep into his lungs, into his bronchial tubes. Within two days, his face had a bluish cast and he was admitted to the hospital.

"It's in God's hands now," the doctor told my mother as she and I sat beside Tony in his hospital crib, listening to his obstructed breathing, watching his little chest heave.

The same doctor who had been so sure there would be no problem, no complications vaccinating Tony when he had a cold was now telling us that she wasn't sure he would live.

Tony had not yet been baptized. Catholics believe that if a baby dies without having been baptized, his soul will go to a place called limbo. He will not be allowed in heaven.

My parents arranged for a priest to come sprinkle a few drops of water on his forehead and baptize him "In the name of the Father, the Son and the Holy Ghost" there in the hospital. Leaning against the wall for support, I crossed myself and silently prayed, St. Anthony, dear friend, please help my baby, please help Tony.

A Proper Baptism

Tony recovered quickly.

A couple of weeks after the emergency baptism, I asked Father Reilly if we could speak in private. He led me into his paper strewn office and I told him about Tony – how I had gotten pregnant in high school and now had a ten month old baby at home with my parents. I asked him if he would baptize my baby.

Normally a baby is baptized within the first few months of his life, but my parents were conflicted because they didn't want to reveal the truth about Tony's birth.

So, with the exception of the hasty, emergency baptism he had received in the hospital, Tony had not yet been properly baptized. I wanted him to have the full ceremony, to be dressed in new white clothes, to be flanked by adoring relatives, to be held in the arms of a godmother.

Father Reilly arranged a private baptism for Tony in an old, historic church in downtown Manhattan, the kind of baptism that rich babies get. Tony was baptized, surrounded by statues of saints, the warm glow of bee's wax candles, the rich colors of stained glass, the elevating aroma of frankincense.

I did not have the courage to challenge my parents' assumption that they would be presented as Tony's mother and father. And so it was that they stood at the baptismal font on either side of the godparents – my mother's good friend, Maria Sanchez, and her husband, Juan. I stood off to the side, next to my younger sister, Sally.

In that church, in that moment, it was enough that Father Reilly knew Tony was mine, that God knew Tony was mine. I was happy that I had made my parents happy. With this baptism, I had finally done something to please them.

The Newman Club Retreat

In late September after Tony was baptized, I signed up for a Newman Club retreat at a scout camp in Westchester. Ours was a weekend of prayer, Catholic camaraderie and good clean fun – hiking, canoeing, singing songs around the campfire. Young Father Reilly was our leader. Dressed in jeans and a sweat shirt, he mingled among us Newman clubbers, encouraging us to participate in the games and sporting events, making sure there were no mopers lurking in the bunks or off walking alone in the woods. To him, it was important that we all be engaged in group activities. He gently kept his eye on us to make sure we were doing just that.

A tall, sandy-haired boy named Jeff started paying attention to me. He asked me to be his canoeing partner, sat next to me on the log in front of the campfire and walked me back to the girls' bunk when it was time to call it a night. We stood outside talking for a while – or at least he was talking. He was telling me all about himself, how he started out at the uptown campus as a Phys Ed major and later switched to History, which meant he was now downtown at Washington Square. He commuted from his parents' home on Long Island. He had a golden lab named Bucko and was a big Mets fan.

At first I thought, Not bad looking for a Catholic boy. His long limbs, square shoulders and well-shaped torso gave him a certain physical grace. His face at rest was handsome but when he spoke, goofiness overtook his features.

"Good night, Jeff. See you for morning prayers," I said.

"Oh, do you have to go in so soon?" he replied, crestfallen.

I said goodnight and left him standing by the door before he could make his move and try to kiss me.

The next morning after prayers and breakfast our weekend retreat came to an end. We boarded the bus and headed back to the city.

On the bus, Jeff, handsome and rugged in a red plaid flannel shirt, snagged the seat next to me. I decided to look beyond his naiveté and give him a chance. Okay, so he had that goofy streak, but he was a good boy, a Catholic boy and I was trying to be good. He was the kind of boy my parents would approve of. Maybe he wasn't Italian, but he was Catholic. Who knew, in their eyes, he might be the kind of guy who'd make a good father for Tony.

After a while, I got tired of hearing about the Mets. I closed my eyes, pretending to sleep. I was just nodding off when Jeff, slowly and gingerly so he wouldn't wake me, put his hand between my legs. Had I been asleep, I would not have felt it. But I wasn't. I knew what he was up to.

What a creep, I thought. What a slimy, sleazy goof-ball.

I was mustering the indignation to push his hand away, fighting against the paralysis that overtook me in situations like this. I was the girl who couldn't say no to boys who put their hands on me, who forced kisses on me. But this time I was almost outraged enough to confront Jeff when he lost his nerve and pulled his hand away.

I kept my eyes closed for the rest of the trip, pretending to sleep. If Jeff had taken his eyes off my body, if he had bothered to study my face, he'd have seen the crimson fury. This redness was the color of anger – at him, but more so at myself.

How could this have happened on a Catholic retreat? Had Jeff sensed something loose, something morally weak about me that led him to touch me there?

I was only pretending to be a good girl. Not only was I not good, I wasn't good at pretending.

So I gave up.

Part II

Brooklyn, NY

Everybody Knew

My mother couldn't bear to live in Westfield anymore. She felt everyone knew.

"They all know and they're making fun of us." She nagged my father until he finally bought into her shame and sold the house.

About one year after Tony was born, we moved to an apartment in Brooklyn, just over the bridge from Manhattan where my father worked and where I was going to school. Ours was considered a luxury apartment in that section of Brooklyn – a doorman was stationed in the lobby and the rooms were big, much bigger than the rooms in Westfield.

The headaches started soon after we moved in. I would lie on my bed in the spacious bedroom I shared with my younger sister, my head pounding. Once in a while, to make myself feel even worse, I would get up to look at myself in the mirror above my dresser. My right eye would be dripping tears, streaked with red. I could see the veins in my right temple throb with each sharp spasm. I would throw myself back down on the bed, cover my eyes with my bent arm and cry. Sometimes I'd scream.

"It's guilt." My mother said I deserved the headaches.

"God's punishing you!" she said.

I needed to get out of that apartment, get away from my parents, their scorn, their cruelty. I daydreamed about running away with my baby son.

Pursuit

I first spotted him through the window of my parents' apartment. He was running down the street. His uneven gait caught my eye. A strange lopsided hop. Like a grasshopper or a kangaroo. Run and then hop. As he ran, he grabbed frantically for his jacket sleeve, in a rush to catch the train, probably late for work.

Something fascinated me, drove me to follow him, to time my movements out of the apartment, down the street to Myrtle Avenue and onto the train so I'd wind up hanging on to the strap next to him.

Did I Love Erik?

Tall and skinny with big, wide feet. "Planchas," my mother called them. Irons.

"The best foot is a big foot," was Erik's slogan. His feet looked particularly big on his skinny frame. He wasn't tall enough for those feet, but he was proud of them. "Prehensile toes," he'd point out to me – long toes, designed by Mother Nature for hanging from tree branches.

I found Erik's feet obscene. He told me mine were too short in

proportion to the width of my legs. "If your feet were bigger, your legs would look thinner," he said.

Big hands to match his feet. Scraggly mustache. Skinny hair. A chipped front tooth. Did I love Erik? Did I know what love is? I didn't even know him when we got married. How can you love someone you don't know? I see now that what attracted me his independence. I loved the idea that he was on his own at age nineteen. Living in a rented room in Brooklyn, working in Manhattan, going to night school at Pratt. Paying his own way, supporting himself, no money from either his mom or his dad.

He ate whatever he wanted, whenever he wanted. Herring in cream sauce. Pumpkin pie. If he felt like having a piece of pumpkin pie, he'd walk down the block to Myrtle Avenue and buy himself a slice. Stuff like that made an impression on me. The only choice I had was what to eat for lunch in the student cafeteria at N.Y.U. And even though I had a choice, tuna was what I chose, day after day. Tuna on Monday, tuna on Tuesday. Tuna, tuna, tuna.

I did not love Erik as a lover. His mouth twisted to one side when he kissed, when he talked, when he laughed. Sometimes I'd turn my head upside down to see how he looked from that angle. But upside down, the twist of his lips seemed even more pronounced.

Upside down or right side up, our mouths did not fit together well, and his lips were hard. He did not love to kiss the way I did, not for as long as I did.

Lawrence Welk

I knew that my mother would find something wrong with any boy I brought home for her to meet. I never expected her to approve of Erik. His was a difficult personality to begin with, and around my family he became even more disagreeable, cruder, haughtier.

His head wobbled like a cocky bird. When he talked to my mother, he held his head back like a rooster, darting his pale blue eyes, never focusing on my mother unless he was zinging her with some thinly veiled barb.

Erik had come over to pick me up one night while my mother sat on the living room couch, watching Lawrence Welk. We were going to see "Chushingura," a Samurai epic at a theater in the East Village.

"You watch that program?" he asked my mother, incredulous. *You must be a moron* was unspoken but implied.

"Come on, Erik, we'll be late for the movie." I rushed him out the door before he had a chance to say more.

Chi Chi

Once, when Erik came to pick me up, baby Tony, his striped shirt wet with drool, was sitting on the living room rug. "Chi chi! Chi chi!" he called to the blue parakeet flapping around in the bird cage on the floor beside him. With each "Chi chi", Tony banged his chubby hands on the top of the cage.

Chico, the parakeet, hopped from perch to perch, letting out an alarmed squawk with each bang. The little copper bells hanging from his plastic mirror jingled.

Bang. Squawk! Jingle.

To me, Tony was the cutest sight in the world, totally absorbing. I was glad he was up and awake so Erik could see how adorable he was and start to get attached to him.

But Erik wasn't one to coo and fuss over babies. He sat and observed Tony with an air of mild curiosity.

He knew Tony was my child. When I told him, soon after we met, it didn't seem to make any difference to him. He didn't treat me like some kind of pariah. Nor did he try to comfort me, sympathize with me, hold my hand or say "Oh, you poor thing, what you must have gone through!"

He just absorbed the information and moved ahead in our relationship.

Dante and Beatrice

In a desperate attempt to scare Erik off, my mother resorted to the ultimate weapon.

Erik stood in my parents' living room with his hands in his back pockets, examining the framed print on the far wall. Dante and Beatrice. A love-struck Dante grasped his wildly beating heart as the beautiful Beatrice strolled past with her companion, Giovanna.

Dante only had eyes for the virginal Beatrice. But Erik was ogling Giovanna who brazenly clutched the folds of her red dress, stretching it tight across the curves of her body.

"Nice set of knockers," Erik muttered.

My mother heard him. She didn't know exactly what he was referring to by "knockers," but the tone of his voice had an unmistakably lewd ring.

That did it. She was going to spill the beans.

"I think you should know, Erik, that Tony – the baby – is Ana's. Before you get too involved with her, I think you should know the truth. She isn't the innocent girl she may appear to be." My mother was hitting it home as hard as she knew how.

"Is that right?" he raised an eyebrow in mock surprise.

Turning to me, he said, "Come on, Ann. We have to make the 5:30 train." He was taking me to Great Neck to meet his mother and stepfather.

He helped me on with my coat, tenderly smoothing down the collar, all for the benefit of my mother. Then he rushed me out the door.

The Blues

The room Erik rented in the brownstone across the street from our apartment was littered with stereo parts – tubes, woofers, tweeters, turntables. From among the dozens of parts he had in his collection, he had assembled one sound system that worked – some of the time. In order to get it to work, there were various switches and buttons that had to be either turned or pushed or pulled. It was such a complicated business, I was afraid to touch it. When I came to his room with him, I'd wait for him to play me one of his blues records.

I could relate to the blues.

Howlin' Wolf, Muddy Waters, John Lee Hooker and my favorite – Jimmy Reed. When Jimmy sang, his sad guitar twanged straight through to my heart.

"Bright lights, big city – Gone to ma baby's head"

How did Erik find this music? I wondered. Certainly not on Murray the K's Swingin' Soiree. And never in places like Westfield, New Jersey. It was too raw, too real.

I started to sing along with Jimmy, "Got me runnin', got me hidin' …"

"Shh!" Erik sat with his eyes closed, his head cocked in the direction of the nearest speaker. "Listen to this riff, just listen," he said, tapping his foot to the beat of the drum.

One night, I noticed a magazine he'd been reading lying open on the floor next to the mattress. I picked it up and read the title of one of the articles, "Freeze, Wait, Reanimate." Goose bumps formed on my arms. "Cryonics is the practice of cryopreserving humans and pets after their legal death. The process is not reversible." Alongside the article was a picture of the man who had undergone the first cryonic suspension.

His body had been quick frozen right after he died! But what about his soul? I wondered. Did his soul freeze, too? What if, instead of freezing, his soul left his body. The reanimated body would be soulless. A zombie.

Erik knew about things I never dreamed existed – civil rights activists, peace marches, "Hiroshima Mon Amour," Peking Duck, the East Village Other. I was fascinated.

Ding Dong

I was not Erik's type, physically. He preferred women with thinner limbs, bigger breasts. He gave me a bottle of vitamin E pills, thinking they would somehow make my breasts bigger. Nourishment. My breasts needed nourishment.

I took the pills. I, too, wished my breasts were bigger.

My mother found the vitamin E pills when she searched my handbag on the sly for evidence of some evil-doing.

Even though the bottle was clearly labeled "Vitamin E," she was sure they were birth control pills. She must have thought I switched bottles.

Too bad they weren't birth control pills.

If I were having sex with Erik, wasn't it better for me to take birth control pills than get pregnant again?

My mother obviously was not thinking along these lines. She confronted me with the evidence.

"Here, look. Look at what I found," she said shaking the glass bottle in my face. "Birth control pills. You whore, you *puta*!"

Her ranting helped set my father off the next night. He knew they were not birth control pills. But just the idea that

Erik bought them for me infuriated him. I had no money of my own. Any money I earned had to be given to my parents who were supporting me and paying for my education. So they knew he bought them.

Another strike against Erik. Not that anything at this point could have changed my father's mind. The more my father knew about Erik, the more he despised him.

The night after my mother found the pills was the night Erik fell asleep snoring on top of me. Waking Erik was never easy and in those days I was not what you would call forceful. I waited for him to wake up, silently lying there beneath him on the thin mattress on the floor of his room. He didn't weigh much more than I did. He wasn't much of a burden, not physically at least. But I was getting anxious about the time. Time was ticking away.

Even a wimp has her breaking point. I started to quietly call Erik's name.

He snorted and turned his head away from me.

"Erik, it's late."

This must have been sweet music to his subconscious with its scorn for structure, its resentment of authority.

I shook his arm gently. "I've got to go now, Erik. Please wake up."

Finally, his eyes opened and he began the long process of stretching, yawning, rising from the mattress, walking naked down the public hallway to the bathroom, peeing, drinking a glass of water, returning to the room, dressing.

By the time we reached the door to my parents' apartment, it was two hours beyond my midnight curfew. My father was waiting up for me. Enraged.

"Hi," I said. "Sorry I'm late, Dad," I was about to make up some story about missing a train but he cut me off.

"Go to your room!" he said, pointing an accusatory finger in the direction of the bedroom like God the Father banishing Eve from Eden.

As I slunk past him, he pushed me forward towards my room, pushed so hard I nearly lost my balance. As I struggled to recover, I heard the sounds of a skirmish behind me.

"Get your hands off her!"

I turned just in time to see Erik lunge at my father. His oversized hands were clenched into fists, ready to punch my father in the jaw.

"Don't you dare!" my father bellowed.

His piercing black eyes stopped Erik dead. Erik averted his gaze, then slowly backed off. With my father's imperious glare following him, Erik turned and left, slamming the door behind him so hard the doorbell chimed. Ding dong.

I wanted to run after Erik, to run away from my father and his wrath, but I knew that if I left that night my parents would never let me come back. They'd never let me return to my baby who was asleep in his crib just down the hall.

For years – for the rest of my father's life, actually – every time Erik's name came up, my father would say, "He threatened me with physical violence."

But *Why* Do You Love Me?

For a guy who claimed to be in love with me, he was harshly critical of my body, and what he called my "Puerto Rican taste." He never complimented me, only told me what was wrong, what didn't quite meet his standards.

We were sitting in a diner on Long Island, in a booth opposite Ronnie and Kevin, Erik's friends from Great Neck High. They were one of those couples who must have been together in previous lives, who seemed as though they had always been together and always would be. I wanted to be loved like that.

"Do you love me?" I asked Erik.

"Yes, yes I love you."

"But *why* do you love me?"

I needed to know why. I needed to know what he found lovable about me. My opinion of myself changed from moment to moment. Sometimes I looked in the mirror and saw a bright, attractive face. Other times, a dopey mug stared back at me. I needed to know why he loved me so that I could love myself.

"I love your velvet vagina," he whispered in my ear.

Later Erik would feel free to tell our deepest, most intimate secrets to even the most casual friends, but that day he whispered his answer in my ear so that Ronnie and Kevin could not hear.

"Wow! It must have been good – look at her smile," Ronnie said.

I hadn't expected it. I didn't know what to think of it. But it sure sounded good, "velvet vagina."

But then I thought, "Don't all women have velvet vaginas? Don't they all feel like velvet inside?"

Proposal in the Subway Station

"Sure, I'll marry you." I had to yell it out over the screech of the subway pulling into the West 4th Street station when Erik asked me to marry him exactly one month after we met.

I figured he meant in a couple of years.

Two days later he told me he had made arrangements for the coming Thursday.

What the heck, I thought. Why not?

Those Scandinavians

By the time I was eighteen, I had heard my mother say over and over, "You'll be a spinster just like those unmarried cousins of your father's. Forty years old, for God's sake, and still living with their parents in Mineola. It must run in the family." My mother considered spinsterhood a congenital disease.

I would counter with, "But Mom, you didn't get married until you were twenty-four!"

"I can see the signs," she'd say. There was no reasoning with a woman who was convinced she could see into the future. "You'll be a spinster, a career woman."

Maybe she said that because I was doing well in school. Too well. I was too serious about my studies. It made my mother nervous. According to her, a woman shouldn't be too brainy. "Men don't marry women who are too well-educated," she said.

When I told her I was getting married, I could sense her great relief.

My mother was never happy because she never let herself be happy. Rather than enjoy her relief, she moved on to her next concern – Erik.

A Norwegian. You know those Scandinavians. They're loose, immoral. They walk around naked. Every chance they get, they strip off their clothes and run naked in the snow. Later, when I got to know Erik's uncles, I found out that she was right. And not just in the snow. He had one uncle who mowed the lawn naked.

This was no prize her daughter was marrying. But her daughter was no prize either. Maybe it was better that her daughter just hurry up, get married, and out of the house.

Thursday

As I was leaving the apartment to go to class on the morning of the wedding, my mother threw a twenty dollar bill at me. "Here, go buy yourself a dress," she said.

I picked up the money from the living room carpet and tucked it in the cloth tote bag I used for carrying my school books ever since the unfortunate incident with the book bag. "Maybe I'll see you at the church tonight," I said to my mother as I headed out the door.

Later that morning, in Italian class I took a seat next to my friend Hillary. Leaning close to her, I said in a low voice, "I'm getting married tonight." I didn't want the Italian professor to hear me. I had a crush on him and wanted to leave my options open just in case things didn't work out and I didn't get married after all.

"Oh, yeah? Who are you planning to marry?" she said, sarcastically. She thought I was kidding.

"Why, Erik. You know, the blond-haired guy who lives across the street from me. I told you about him," I said, not surprised that she couldn't guess. "I'm serious. We're getting married tonight. Can you come?"

I liked the fact that people were shocked.

"You're getting married just like that?" My friend Joan couldn't believe it when I told her in the Geology Lab. "On a school night? Instead of going to the library to work on your anthropology assignment? You're marrying some guy you've only known for a month?"

After classes that day, I walked up to S. Klein on the Square. Where else could I find a dress for twenty dollars?

S. Klein on the Square

Even at S. Klein, finding a dress that was cheap enough and still looked okay on me wasn't easy. It was hard work picking through the sale bins, searching through crowded rows of wrinkled dresses hanging lopsided on metal racks in the back corner of the store.

I started to feel dizzy. I started to sweat. I sank to the floor. I was pregnant again, but just a few weeks pregnant so I wasn't aware of it yet. No period had been missed, no sore breasts yet, no swollen belly. Fainting was the first sign. But I chalked it up to the heat in the store, the lack of ventilation, the pressure to find a dress in time to meet Erik in the office building uptown.

I fanned myself with a manila folder I had in my tote bag. Gradually my head started to clear. With one hand on the dress rack, I pulled myself up and returned to the clearance bins. I found a navy blue dress with white piping, marked way down – probably left over from the spring collection. It fit me, so I bought it.

I met Erik at the architect's office on West 44th Street where he worked as a draftsman. He took me to Woolworths and we shopped for a ring. 'A fake gold ring for a make believe marriage,' I thought.

The ring may have been fake but Erik was serious about the marriage. He even paid for the ceremony.

A Family

It was good that Erik was crazier about me than I was about him. I figured that way I couldn't be hurt.

I was hoping that once we settled down, once we could afford a small apartment instead of living in a rented room, we could take the baby with us. We'd be a family. But I hadn't shared my dream with Erik yet. Maybe I was afraid he'd say no.

Where Are the Flowers?

It was a cold, damp December night but Erik was wearing only a thin sports coat. The sleeves were a bit short and I could see the face of his watch without having to ask him to push up his sleeve. 7:20. We were late for our own wedding! We ran up the subway stairs and down the block. As we rounded the corner, we saw our wedding guests huddled together outside the entrance to the Unitarian Church – Erik's parents (two sets of them), my parents, Erik's uncles and their wives, his friends from Great Neck, and Joan, my friend from Geology class.

They had waited outside the door, hesitant to enter. Maybe they thought our wedding was just a big joke, or else that we had gotten cold feet.

I apologized. "I'm so sorry you had to wait. We had to take a local, the express train was packed," I lied.

Erik acted as if there were nothing wrong, nothing unusual in a couple being late for their wedding. He strode through the door and turned to me and our guests. "Come on, come on," he said, impatiently waving his arm to herd us inside.

I'd never been inside a Protestant Church before. I was jarred by the starkness of the red brick walls. I looked around for the altar but all I found was a wooden podium. Folding chairs instead of carved wooden pews. No windows.

But what was that in the niche behind the minister? A statue of St. Anthony holding the infant Jesus, a white dove on his shoulder. Anthony of Padua, the saint I prayed to when I was pregnant, the saint I named my son after. There he was, the only statue in the chapel of the Unitarian church, watching over me as I married Erik.

We stood awkwardly side by side, not knowing what we were supposed to do. Erik kept shifting his weight from one foot to the other. He had his hands in his pockets to keep from fidgeting. I had the feeling that I wasn't really there. It wasn't really me in the navy blue dress. I was a disembodied waif, drifting high overhead. A spectator.

Where are the flowers? I wondered. What kind of wedding is this with no flowers?

My Father

Only my father thought to bring a camera – his Polaroid. He used the camera for work. He was a lawyer for a shipping corporation and he used the Polaroid to create visual proof to present in court. Did he bring it to the Unitarian Church to have proof that I was really getting married? Whatever the reason, he took some photos. Just a few. Polaroid film is expensive.

Later, I learned my father sent for a copy of our marriage certificate to keep as further proof that his daughter was legally married. Maybe he thought the wedding was a hoax.

I think that in my father's eyes Erik and I were play acting, toying with something he took seriously. A real marriage was for the rest of your life. My father's own marriage was a disaster but he took it seriously and it lasted until the day he died. Fifty-three years.

My Mother

My mother, stiff and unsmiling, sat on the edge of her seat with arms folded. In the Polaroid shots my father took, none of our guests are smiling, only Erik and I have smiles on our faces – sheepish smiles, but smiles none the less. If it weren't for our smiles, you'd think it was a funeral. Stern faces. Dark clothes, even on the bride.

My mother wiped tears from her eyes. I knew they were not tears of joy, but tears of anguish, of futility, of fear. What would become of this travesty of a marriage? My mother – the shortest one in the group, barely five feet tall, the little Puerto Rican mother – stopped dabbing her tears long enough to push her skirt down over her knees. Little, sad, unsmiling mother

My older sister, still in nursing school, did not yet know that I was getting married. And the younger one was at home in the apartment in Brooklyn taking care of the baby. My parents would not allow my younger sister to attend the wedding. They made it seem shameful, despicable. Dirty, sinful. They would never willingly expose their younger daughter to this mockery.

Helen

As we assembled for the group shot, Erik's mother, Helen, looked around at her three brothers who were seated behind her and said, "We Swenssens must really believe in marriage because we've all been married more than once." She laughed lustily. "Carsten, Dell and I are on our second marriages. And the baby of the family, my brother Bron over there, he outdid us all. He's already on this third!"

Helen was seated in one of the folding chairs grouped together in the chapel. Her husband, Dan, sat next to her. Off to the right, leaning against the brick wall stood Erik's father, Bill Hansen, silent and specter-like with his white hair and ghostly pale skin. "Stretch" they called him because he looked like he'd been hanging from a trapeze too long. His current wife, Hazel, a short woman in a silly flowered hat, stood cross-armed in front of him, the topmost flower just barely reaching his Adam's apple. Guarding him. From what?

Hazel must have sensed that the flame of desire for Helen still burned in her husband's heart. And she was right. Many years later, after Dan left Helen and after Hazel died, Bill called Helen to suggest they get together again. "For a roll in the hay," was how he put it.

The "Reception"

After the Unitarian minister spoke, after the certificate was signed, after the photos were taken, the wedding party milled around not knowing what to do next, where to go. Go home? Was this it? Shouldn't there be more to this wedding – more than a "play" ring? A bride in navy blue? A few Polaroid shots?

Dan, Erik's stepfather, saved the day. He invited the wedding guests for drinks at a neighborhood bar a couple of blocks away.

Dan's generosity had its limits, however. My father stubbornly refused to pay for any part of this wedding, including the drinks, so the impromptu reception at the local bar did not last long.

A Cup of Coffee and a Snack

Erik and I, now husband and wife, stopped at my parents' apartment before going to his rented room for our first married night together. I tossed a change of clothes, my toothbrush, makeup into a beat up cardboard suitcase.

"What about your nightgown?" my mother asked. "Aren't you going to pack your nightgown?"

A sardonic twist appeared on Erik's mouth, exposing his chipped tooth. "Oh, she won't be needing a nightgown," he said.

Erik scoffed at nightgowns and pajamas, made fun of people who wore them. He believed in sleeping nude. "In the raw," was how he put it.

He was sitting at my parents' dining room table, in no rush to leave. No rush at all. He asked for coffee. "You wouldn't happen to have something sweet, pumpkin pie maybe, that I could have with my coffee?" His smile was full of mischief.

My mother sliced a piece of coffee cake, pushed it off the serving knife onto a plate and slammed it down in front of her new son-in-law.

Time passed. I wondered if Erik was planning to sit there all night.

My mother kept wiping the table with her napkin even though there were no crumbs or drips to clean up. I could imagine her thinking, *This is their wedding night. Why isn't he anxious to get home?*

My mother's anxiety infected me. I nervously tried to get Erik to finish his cake.

"Maybe we should leave now, Erik." Looking at him sitting there cocksure at the head of my parents' dining room table, I realized full well the message he was sending to my parents. With his unhurried attitude, he was letting them know that sex was nothing new for these newlyweds.

Before leaving, I walked down the hallway to the bedroom where Tony was sleeping, leaned over his crib and kissed his forehead. "Sleep well, my little baby. We'll be together soon," I whispered.

The Gold Cross

Erik believed in sleeping naked. He even insisted that I take off my gold cross, the one my Uncle Dominic found in the sands he sifted at Coney Island before the days of metal detectors.

Erik hung the cross on the wall at the head of the bed. Then he laughed. For him, hanging the cross on the wall was an act of defiance against God the Father. God, in whom he did not believe. How can you defy what you do not believe exists?

And I, lying there exposed and uncomfortable on Erik's mattress, felt like a fallen soul, beyond forgiveness. At least part of me felt like that. The other part felt excited and wanted to experience the life that Erik was offering to me.

How Could You Not Like Dogs?

One Saturday afternoon, we were walking by a pet shop on Myrtle Avenue. In those days the elevated train, the Myrtle Avenue El, was still running, still shuttling people to the downtown area where they'd catch another train to Manhattan, or into the bowels of Bedford Stuyvesant.

There were puppies in the window of the pet shop and I stopped to watch them, to see them play, to hear their little puppy barks, high pitched yaps. So cute. Someday I wanted to have a puppy of my own.

"I don't like dogs," Erik said.

"How could you not like dogs?" I turned to look at him a little closer. He shrugged and kept on walking.

He must be kidding, I concluded. It's impossible not to like dogs – as impossible as not liking spaghetti or chocolate or babies.

How could I have married a guy who doesn't like dogs?

I Hate it When You Sing

In elementary school and later in High School, I used to think I could sing. My mother thought I could, too, and so did my older sister. "You have a beautiful voice," they said.

In those days in Westfield, the three of us were fooled into believing I could sing. But when I tried out for the Westfield Warblers – an exclusive girls' singing group – my High School choir master wasn't fooled.

"You, you and you – you can go now," she said pointing her finger at me and two other girls.

I wasn't told why I was asked to leave. I wanted to believe that my voice was so lovely and so strong that the choir teacher knew I should be part of that exclusive group. No need to keep me there in the music room with Melissa Bird at the piano. I went home confident – as confident as I knew how to be.

A couple of days later, the list of the chosen few was posted. My name wasn't on it.

I sang with the big choir – the more the merrier with voices like mine.

I once asked Erik to sing for me. He sang a couple of lines from a blues song. His singing sounded like a comic imitation of a white man imitating a black man.

"No, come on. Be serious," I said.

"I *am* being serious."

Erik didn't sing much. He left it to the singers to sing, on the records, on the radio, in the concert halls. He didn't want me to sing either. When I would sing in the apartment, join in with the singers on the radio, or belt one out on my own, a capella, he'd say, "Come on, you're ruining the song." Or "Stop singing. I hate it when you sing."

How can you stay married to a man who stops you from singing?

And he didn't like dogs, for goodness sake.

How can you be happy if you can't sing? How can you be happy without a dog? How can you be happy without your baby?

How Could I Know I was Pregnant?

We'd only known each other for one month when we got married, so how could I know? Erik was using condoms, but within the first few weeks of our marriage, I could no longer fool myself – I had to face the fact that I was pregnant.

Erik and I knew from the snide remarks we'd overheard from our relatives and friends that they figured I was pregnant when we got married. Why else would a couple rush into marriage after only one month?

"We'll show them," Erik and I said to each other. "We'll show them we didn't have to get married, we just wanted to."

When I realized I was pregnant again, my heart sank. I had married Erik to make a home for my son, Tony. But he was still with my parents. I had not yet accomplished what I had set out to do. I needed more time. Why couldn't this new baby have waited?

Baby Grand Piano

I'd heard women say you should not lift heavy objects or do strenuous exercise when you're pregnant. My mother told me she had miscarried her first child simply by reaching too high. She'd been hanging drapes while my father was at work. A few days later she lost her baby.

I started lifting heavy things – a carton of books, Erik's power saw, the tree stumps we used for kitchen chairs – and when none of the heavy objects in our own apartment produced results, I looked around my parents' apartment. One afternoon while Tony was napping in the bedroom and my mother was downstairs loading laundry into one of the washing machines in the basement, I crawled under the baby grand piano. I squatted there, pressing my hands flat against the under side of the piano. I pushed and strained against it like Atlas holding up the world. But the piano didn't budge and neither did the baby inside me.

Out of breath, holding my belly, I lay sprawled on my back under the piano. "Okay, I give up," I said to the tenacious little life that was so determined to be born. "It's not that I don't love you, it's just that I have other things I need to do right now. Couldn't you wait for me to finish school and convince Erik and my parents that Tony should live with us?"

I was beginning to lose hope that my dream would ever become reality. Erik never seemed to take it seriously. He acted as if my wanting Tony would pass, disappear like a bad mood if he just ignored it.

When I tried to talk to my father about taking Tony to live with me, I wound up sobbing. "Look at yourself," he would say. "Look at your life! What kind of a mother would you be?" Like a sledge hammer his words crushed any confidence I might have had in my ability to be a good mother. Standing there crying, I saw myself as he saw me – childish, stupid, foolish.

Fried Shit

Chop up onions, chop up green pepper. Fry up the onions, the pepper, the chopped meat, some potatoes – if you've got them. Throw in some canned tomato sauce, spices and anything else you have in the refrigerator, and voila! you've got yourself some fried shit. Erik would make it for dinner when we were first married. I could not cook, so he took the helm, manned the stove. Every night the same routine. Fried shit.

There were some nights in the middle of our first winter together when there was no heat in the building because the utility bill had not been paid. On those nights I would sleep with Erik on the communal kitchen table in front of the gas stove with all four burners and the oven lit.

Staten Island

It wasn't long after Erik and I married that my parents moved with Tony to Staten Island. The ferry to Manhattan was only a couple of blocks from their apartment building. My father could walk from the terminal to his office on Rector Street. No subway. A substantial advantage. But the real reason behind the move was to put some distance – a body of water – between me and my child.

When I married Erik and moved into his rented room across the street from my parent's apartment, I could walk over to see Tony any time I wanted, as long as my parents were speaking to me. As long as they would open the door, I could go and see my Tony, take him out to the playground, watch him ride his little red tricycle.

Tony was not yet three years old but already he had the serious demeanor, the furrowed, worried brow of my father.

"I love you, little man," I'd say to him, kissing his forehead. "Please don't worry. Everything is going to work out for us."

Willoughby Avenue

When we found the apartment on Willoughby Avenue, I loved it at first sight. Mrs. Rosenberg, the little white-haired landlady in the flowered house dress, had shown us the parlor apartment with high ceilings, carved woodwork, French doors, tall windows. Such elegance, I thought, deciding exactly where we would put the baby grand piano that my parents had been keeping for me in their apartment till then.

The apartment was a bit more expensive than what Erik had in mind, but I wanted to live there. He should never have taken me to see it if he knew it cost too much.

Lethargy

The new baby was there inside me on that bed when lethargy took hold of me and I could not get up. I could not lift myself from the bed. I had no energy.

I must have complained to my mother.

"I don't know what's wrong with me, Mom. I find it harder and harder to drag myself to class."

She must have told my sister, Ines. Ines told her husband, Lou who worked in the pharmaceutical business. Lou Rossa to the rescue with pills to fix me right up.

I took the pills. They made me feel better, they made my mind active. Now when I lay on the mattress, my mind raced. I saw myself going to school, studying, cleaning, shopping, walking, riding the subway. In my mind I was taking care of everything. I saw myself charged with endless energy. But I didn't do too well at NYU that semester. I didn't do much of anything except lie on the mattress on the floor.

What Fun!

We were the only ones in Erik's circle of friends from Great Neck who were married and had an apartment of our own. So his friends came over often.

One Friday night, Erik and three buddies from Great Neck were crowded together on our mattress, lying on their backs, their pants down, their legs curled up against their chests, only dingy white jockey shorts covering their butts. They reached around their thighs and held lit matches by their cracks, straining to push out gas. Poof! The head of the match exploded into flame. What fun! Like trained seals at the aquarium, they chortled with glee.

The only drawback was burn holes in their jockey shorts. But they didn't seem to mind.

Inside me, the baby I would name Luke was just starting his life as I sat on the bedroom floor watching his father and his buddies light their farts.

One of Erik's friends, Larry Szabo, a sleazy pre-med student, walked over to the corner where I was sitting, my arms wrapped around my legs, my chin resting on my knees.

Larry offered me a beer. Just the smell of it made me want to puke. I shook my head no, too depressed to talk.

"Pretty soon you'll have two children to deal with," Larry said, smiling. He found humor in this situation.

'I'll have three,' I thought, still determined to claim my right to be Tony's mother, and raise him the way normal mothers raise their sons.

It was all getting so complicated. Now I had to take a ferry to go see Tony. The last time I did, I started to feel queasy, dizzy. The lurching motion of the ferry had sent me rushing to the ladies' room three or four times before the trip was over.

Mrs. Rosenberg

Our landlady, Mrs. Rosenberg, seemed fond of me but suspicious of Erik. She'd heard too many thuds, too many rumbles, too much crying and yelling.

Mrs. Rosenberg lived in the basement apartment below us. At night as she sat in front of her TV, she must have overheard many fights between the young couple upstairs – me, running for cover in the bathroom, slamming the door behind me, Erik kicking in the door, breaking the lock.

She must have heard me cry out in pain when he hit me with a two by four, about the size of a baseball bat. Like a baseball player warming up at the plate, he had swung it at me, making contact with the back of my left thigh. I'd seen it coming and had turned my body away from him, instinctively protecting the fetus that was nested inside me.

Once, towards the end of my pregnancy, I was taking a shower when Erik snuck into the bathroom with his camera and snapped a photo of me.

"This is to remind me never to get you pregnant again," he said with that snaggle-toothed smirk on his face. "You're fat and ugly!'

I screamed at him, thrashing my arms like a windmill, "Get out! Get out! Get out of here!" Mrs. Rosenberg must have heard me.

Once he pushed me out of bed. That may not seem so awful – falling from a bed to the floor isn't such a long fall, and a young person – a twenty year old, say, could survive that fall unscathed, walk away in no worse shape. But our bed was high up on a platform. And underneath the platform was my baby grand piano. So when Erik pushed me out of bed, I first hit the keys of the piano, scraping my side against them, then glanced off the piano bench and landed with a thud on the hard wood floor.

Why did he push me? I was crying, crying for Tony. I was telling Erik I wanted Tony to live with us. I wanted Luke and Tony to grow up together as brothers. I wanted to really be Tony's mother, to raise him, feed him, help him on with his jacket in the morning and walk him to school.

Erik wanted me to stop crying so he pushed me out of bed.

Why I decided I liked Pete Sultanis

Erik had a friend named Pete Sultanis, a tall, fleshy, smart guy, good in math and sciences. He used to say that if you're driving somewhere and you don't know where you are – you should drive faster so you can get out of the lost place sooner.

It took a while for me to like Pete because he was such a guy's guy. All I had experienced of him was his bawdy joking around with the raunchy crew that made up Erik's circle of friends from high school. They were a pack – like wild dogs (except wild dogs don't light their own farts).

Pete was Erik's best man at our wedding. A year-and-a-half later, I was sitting in my kitchen with him. He'd come over to see Erik, but Erik wasn't home yet, so I offered him a grilled cheese with bacon.

I fried the bacon brown and crisp, pressing it, stabbing it, turning it until each piece was uniformly crisp, until all the fatty blisters had fried to golden. I lined up the bacon strips side by side on a piece of paper towel.

I wanted to dump all the slimy fat in the pan down the drain. When Erik wasn't watching, that's what I did.

My mother used to save bacon fat in a metal coffee can which was kept in the refrigerator. She'd use the fat to cook with. I found the can of white fat so repulsive that when my mother and father weren't around I'd dump the bacon fat down the drain.

I looked at Pete and said, "I know you're not supposed to dump the fat down the drain but ..."

Pete said, "Actually, if you put the hot water on full force to clear the drain of the fat, then it's okay ... and, hey, Ann, this sandwich is delicious!"

It's okay, I told myself, I just have to make sure all the fat gets flushed down – then it's okay! What I'm doing is okay. Pete thinks so, and he's smart.

Maybe Erik and my parents are wrong about me.

My Mother-in-law, My Idol

The first time I met my mother-in-law, Helen, she had invited me to dinner in Great Neck. This was before Erik and I were married.

She was wearing a short skirt – much shorter than any skirt I had ever seen a mother wear. Her knees and a couple of inches of thigh were exposed. She wore forest green tights. Her hair hung softly in a shoulder-length pageboy.

I had never met a woman like Helen. She laughed from her belly at any good joke, even off-color ones. My mother would have scowled if she had heard such jokes. My mother had permed hair and kept her skirts pulled down tightly below her knees. Keeping her skirt and her daughter's skirts down was a major preoccupation. She would watch us closely and critically when we were in male company – like a *dueña*, making sure propriety was upheld.

Helen didn't smile all the time and nod like so many women automatically do in a social situation. If she didn't feel like smiling, she didn't.

She wore her hair the way she wanted, even if it wasn't in fashion. Once when she was preparing to go to a fancy social event, the premiere of one of Her husband's documentaries, her friends convinced her to get her hair done. In those days, the style for a woman of Helen's age was a variation on the flip. The hair was parted in the middle, teased into two rounded hills on the crown of the head, then draped over the ears in long S curves. A thick layer of hair spray kept every strand in place.

"I looked like a water buffalo," said Helen. She told me she ducked into alleys and doorways as she walked home to avoid being seen by anyone she knew. Once home, she ran upstairs to the bathroom and soaked her head.

Martini Time

Helen never apologized for her martini consumption. She wasn't one to sneak drinks. She mixed martinis out in the open for all to see, plunking a green olive into the long stemmed glass, foggy from the freezer, cold and icy.

Her strong Norwegian body could handle the hardiest drink. She remained steady, regardless of the ratio of gin to vermouth.

"Helen, are you really going to have another one?" her husband would whine, exasperated.

"Why not?" Helen's voice deepened.

What of it? was her silent message to the people who would lift an eye brow at the number of martinis glasses emptied in a mere two hours. She would raise the glass to her lips, tipping it with such pleasure, you'd be tempted to have a martini, too – if you thought you could handle it. Martinis looked delicious flowing through Helen's lips.

Helen would sit at her kidney shaped table in Great Neck, her papers, notebooks, red pens, poems and stories spread out in neat disarray. She was a tidy housekeeper but hers was not a regimented order. I felt at home there sitting on her sofa, leafing through the latest issue of the *New Yorker*, sipping tea from a china cup. She had a sure eye for beauty and surrounded herself with exquisite objects – polished teak furniture handcrafted by her brothers, delicate porcelain vases, lush Kashmiri carpets.

She wrote every day. She didn't care if others thought it was a waste of time, a great pretension. If she ever entertained any self-doubts, her desire to write over powered those niggling thoughts, just as her love for martinis was stronger than the sneers, the whining, the arched eyebrows.

I admired Helen and wanted to be just like her.

Madman Behind the Wheel

Helen didn't drive. She did her shopping and ran her errands around the village of Great Neck on her bike. I imagine she didn't drive for the same reason I didn't: she was afraid. People get maimed and killed in cars and by cars.

For the same reason, fear, Helen wouldn't ride in Erik's car. That was the rule. No talking her out of it.

"No, I won't be a passenger in any car Erik is driving," she would say, her arms crossed firmly against her chest.

Erik was a madman behind the wheel. Being the driver gave him his chance to scare people. He held them captive, glued to their seats. With the car speeding down the street, screeching around corners, they'd think twice about opening a car door and jumping out. And even if they did bail out – hey, that might be fun, too – for him!

He couldn't bear to be stuck behind some slow moving vehicle – a semi-trailer, say. He had to pass it, even if he couldn't see oncoming traffic. To him, it was more of a thrill to hold your breath and take your chances.

His mother called it a Norwegian death wish, left over in his DNA from Viking ancestors.

Once, on the Long Island Expressway, heading out from Brooklyn to Great Neck to visit his mother, Erik and I found ourselves behind two big rigs. After weaving left and right to see where he might pass, Erik aimed his old beat-up sports car, a black Triumph, between the two monster trucks, creating a middle lane on the two lane highway. It took a moment for the incredulous truck drivers to react. They shook their fists, pounded their horns, blew their whistles. You could tell they'd never seen a driver as wild as the lunatic in the black Triumph.

A Name for the Baby

As Luke grew bigger inside me, so did my love for him – or her. They didn't have sonograms in those days so I didn't know until I actually laid eyes on him that he was Luke and not Lilli, or whatever name we would have chosen if our baby had been a girl.

Erik was lobbying for Carol, the name of the girl he'd been seeing just before he met me. But there was no way I was going to have a daughter named after my husband's old girlfriend. I liked the name Lilli, but Erik considered it just another manifestation of my bad taste.

Although a name for a girl was still up in the air, we were sure about the name Luke. I'd been looking at pamphlet from the maternity clinic – "A Name for Your New Baby." Nothing grabbed me until I reached the name Luke. Yes! Luke was it.

"Oh, no! How could you do that to your child?" said Kevin and Ronnie who thought it sounded like a for a hillbilly. Those were the days before Cool Hand Luke, before American mothers-to-be considered Luke an acceptable name for their sons.

When I thought of the name Luke, images of intensity, brightness, the light of the sun filled my mind.

Perfect

How perfect he looked when the doctor held him up for me to see – red, yes, but perfect – chubby, round, nine-and-a-half pounds. I had the cutest, most perfect baby ever born – beside Tony, that is.

He sprang from me. Jet propelled. The doctor caught him the way you catch a football, with both arms. Luckily, the doctor was young, quick, athletic – a good catch.

How different Luke was from Tony, who had thought about it long and hard: Is this what I really want? Is leaving the womb a wise move? Tony had to be coaxed out with forceps.

Helen, Luke's grandma, had her first glimpse of Luke in the hospital just after he was circumcised. The nurse was wheeling him back to the nursery in his little white cart.

"I just saw my grandson," She told me, sitting down in the chair next to my hospital bed. "He was furious!" She laughed – not because she thought there was humor in being circumcised. She was overwhelmed by the strength, the life force of this newborn.

When Erik first saw Luke, he said, "He's not cute, he's funny looking."

Erik was lying next to me on the hospital bed, clutching at my hard breasts. He had closed the curtains around us and instead of staying seated in the chair beside me, he had climbed into bed. He loved to make a scene, to shock.

He lay there next to me in black pants and white shirt. He'd come straight from work to the hospital to visit me and see his baby.

"Mr. Hanson!" the nurse cried out when she came in to check up on all the new mothers in the room. "Get up out of that bed and leave your poor wife alone for a while."

No Comb

I had cried in the hospital. I had laughed and cried. One minute laughing, the next crying. I was crying when Helen came to visit and sat down in the chair next to me.

My hair was a wild mess. I didn't have a comb. My husband had left me and our baby there in the hospital with nothing of our own – no clothes, no toothpaste, no comb.

Helen opened her neat, organized hand bag and looked inside – a folded white cloth handkerchief, a shiny black wallet with a metal clasp in the shape of a hand, a small journal, a pen, lipstick and a comb. She handed me the comb so I could work on my wild nest of hair, untangle the knots. Her hair was thin and straight. The fine-toothed comb glided smoothly through it. But not through mine. I cried from the pain of pulling my hair as the comb found the knots. I cried because I had been left in the hospital without my own comb. I cried because my baby didn't have a hat to wear when he left the hospital on Easter Sunday.

"Don't worry, sweetie," Helen said. "I'll come back tomorrow with baby clothes and a hat."

The next day she handed me a little blue knitted cap, an heirloom, handmade by Luke's great grandmother, Olga Jennsen, when she was pregnant with her first son.

Dan's Theory

Helen's second husband, Dan, had a theory about mothers and their sons. Dan, who only had daughters, used to say that when doctors deliver baby boys, they also perform some type of cranial surgery on the mother. They remove part of her brain along with the baby. Without that part, the mother cannot think logically about her son. She will never be rational when it comes to her boy. She will never be able to see him as anything but her adorable boy child.

Rag Doll

After I gave birth to Luke, I spent one week at Helen's. I stayed with Luke in the room that was once Erik's bedroom. Sometimes Luke slept in a wicker basket on the floor near the bed but mostly he lay by my side, nursing. For most of the day, I held him close to me. This baby is mine – really, really mine, I thought. My father, my mother, no one can take him from me.

Luke and I were glued together. I rarely left the room.

Toward the end of the week, Helen had guests over for lunch – a female friend and her three-year-old daughter. I heard them talking downstairs but I had no intention of joining them. I was too much in love with the baby lying next to me.

Helen came upstairs to invite me down. "I'm worried about you," she said. "Cooped up in this bedroom all week long." Maybe she thought I had post partum depression. "The baby's asleep. It will do you good."

I didn't want to leave the baby but I couldn't say no. I loved my mother-in-law and wanted to please her. "Okay," I said, and returned my sleeping baby to the wicker basket.

Who knows what was talked about downstairs at Helen's oak table. I wasn't much interested. I was only interested in Luke.

I heard him cry.

I bolted from my chair and ran toward the stairs. The little girl stood at the top landing, holding Luke in front of her like a rag doll. He was screaming now. I leaped up the stairs, taking them two at a time and scooped the baby up.

When I got him back to bed, I gave him my breast to sooth him. But my milk started gushing out, it wouldn't stop. Luke almost choked. He couldn't suck fast enough, milk dribbled down his face. The milk soaked the bed sheets, the pillows, the mattress.

Tony's Nose

I felt close to Helen. One day we were sitting in her kitchen in Great Neck. Luke was in my arms. Together, we examined him, admiring his hands, his feet, his nose – deciding which side of the family each part came from. The feet and hands were Erik's. The nose was mine.

"I know the nose is mine because my son Tony has the same one." There, now she knows, I thought, keeping my eyes on the baby, waiting to hear her reaction, afraid to look up to see the expression on her face.

"You have another son?" she asked, after a few heart beats of silence.

"Yes," I said. "But I wasn't married. I got pregnant in High School and now my mother and father are raising him. They're pretending to be his parents, but he's really mine." I squeezed my index finger into Luke's clenched hand and felt his firm grip. I couldn't look into my mother-in-law's eyes.

Helen moved closer to me and brushed the hair back from my eyes. She caught my gaze and said softly, "That must be so difficult for you."

I burst into tears. "I want him with me," I cried. "I want to be his mother. I want Luke to be his brother…"

Helen cradled me in her arms, rocking me and the baby.

A Red Crib

Luke had been cooped up in a carriage for almost two months when we finally got a crib for him. I bought the carriage, an English pram, when I was pregnant, knowing it was impractical. I didn't care. I wanted to wheel my baby in an elegant carriage. I blew all our money on the pram – there was no money left to buy a crib, so my parents gave me the crib that was once Tony's. They had painted it white; I repainted it red.

Luke was a big, active baby who resented being confined. He cried in his carriage, in his red crib and even in his Jolly Jumper, the little swing Erik's Uncle Carsten bought him, guaranteed to give baby hours of fun and mother the break she so desperately needs.

Crying. It seemed he was always crying. He didn't sleep, not for long anyway. I remember reading in Dr. Spock that a newborn infant rarely stays awake more than half an hour at a stretch. I kept going back to that paragraph, rereading it, wanting it to be true.

Luke would stay awake crying for hours, or he would have cried if I hadn't been holding him, rocking him, pacing back and forth with him across the bedroom floor, between the

English pram and the wooden platform bed Erik had built for us where he lay sleeping, grinding his teeth.

Now, in his red crib, Luke was free to turn over, to peer out the sides of the crib and watch his parents fight, watch his father throw a jelly jar at his mother, watch his mother cry, watch his mother cut holes in the toes of his father's socks when his father was out of the house.

Luke wore me out. He was so full of energy, so strong, so demanding. I didn't have time to think about Tony, much less visit him.

More than once when I was pregnant with Luke, he kicked me so violently I fell off the wooden platform bed onto the floor. One afternoon in Physics class, his kicks sent me flying off the lab stool.

I remember trying to feed Luke mashed carrots from a baby food jar. He was propped up in his baby carrier on the kitchen table – red-faced, crying, angrily kicking with his chubby legs.

Watching him, I was overcome with his utter vulnerability. If I decided one day that I couldn't take his crying anymore and just walked out the front door, leaving him there, he would perish. Maybe if he knew he was totally dependent on me, he wouldn't have cried so much, he wouldn't have pushed me so hard, he wouldn't have tired me so. Or maybe he did know and that was why he was so furious.

How could I think such things? Was my father right? Was I really incapable of being a good mother?

Marjory Kleinman

Dan's sister, Marjory Kleinman, was a pediatrician and since we were family, she kindly agreed to be Luke's pediatrician, free of charge.

Marjory lived in the depths of Brooklyn, way down along Flatbush Avenue. Erik and I lived at the other end, close to Manhattan. We brought Luke to Marjory for his check ups.

I was young – only twenty – and could not readily appreciate good looks in older people. And although Marjory Kleinman was well into her sixties at the time, she was so attractive that even I, in the ignorance of youth, could see she was lovely. And she was fond of Luke.

She gave Luke all his shots, doctored him through the attacks of bronchitis he suffered as a baby, weighed him, measured him, charted his growth.

She called the blanket he clutched when he sucked his thumb, a *shmata*. She suggested that I cut it up into pieces so parts of it could be washed and still leave him something to hold on to. Later, when he learned to talk, he called it his "ketta" – short for "blanquetta," a word I made up. Luke talked early.

Marjory loved to test his reflexes, his awareness. He followed her flashlight with his gaze when he was just a few weeks old.

"This baby's a genius!" she declared. Naturally I was crazy about Marjory. Naturally I felt she was a wonderful doctor. Wise. Insightful.

Convinced that the baby lying on the table in front of her had great potential, she gave him her undivided attention. "How's my favorite guy doing?" she asked him during one of her examinations. She was leaning over him while she listened to his heart beat, tapped his belly, unpinned his diaper and felt his scrotum, checked to see that his testicles were descending properly.

A geyser of clear baby pee shot up from his penis into Marjory's open mouth.

"Oh!" she cried. "Oh, no!" She covered her mouth first with her right, then her left hand. With both hands over her mouth, she ran out of the examination room.

Olive Wamsley

Mrs. Wamsley lived in the basement of the brownstone at the end of our block. She had scraggly hair that looked like she'd given up washing and combing it years ago, big saggy bosoms, and rolls of fat around her middle. She always wore black – black blouse, black skirt, black socks, black sneakers.

She sat in her gray metal folding chair surveying the block, shaking her fists at the neighborhood kids, pointing at people as they passed.

"Ey, you, where'd you get that 'at? You look like a bloody clown in it!" she'd say in her Cockney accent.

All that arm motion would cause her blouse to creep up above the waistband of her skirt and flap loosely in the breeze until she tucked it back in, grunting with the effort.

On weekends when the weather was warm, I would put Luke in his stroller and take him to the playground. One mild autumn day, on our way down the block, we passed Mrs. Wamsley sitting on her folding chair outside her building.

Luke was squirming, trying to get out of the stroller. He wanted me to carry him. He stretched his arms out pathetically, kicked his feet against the frame of the stroller, crying "Cawy,

Mama, cawy!" He let out a scream so high pitched and loud, it could have broken an ear drum.

"I'll call the coppers on ya, I will!" Mrs. Wamsley yelled. She heaved her bottom up from her chair and waddled towards us. "They'll put ya' in the clink where ya' belong!"

Oh, God, I thought. She's going to have me arrested for child abuse!

It must have seemed to her that I was being cruel, not picking Luke up, letting him scream. A bad mother.

But as the old lady came closer, I could see that it was Luke she was shaking her crooked finger at.

"Ya'd best behave, Mista, or I'll have ya trown in da slamma!" The sight of her, all in black, looming over him, shut Luke right up. He sank back into his stroller and remained quiet for the rest of our walk.

Mrs. Wamsley used to brag that she could pee into a coke bottle. She'd demonstrate right there on the street for anyone who cared to watch. She'd put the coke bottle down on the sidewalk between her feet and stand over it, carefully calculating the exact position of her body in relation to the thin neck of the coke bottle. Then she'd let loose.

If crazy Mrs. Wamsley could make Luke behave, why couldn't I?

Corina Williams

Corina and Jimmie Williams lived in the brownstone next to ours. They had seven daughters, ranging in age from six to seventeen. On Saturday evenings Corina's daughters would wash their hair in preparation for church the next day. During the warm summer months, they would sit cross-legged on the grass in the backyard in front of Corina, perched stately as a queen in a chair brought outside from the kitchen. With the speed and dexterity that comes from years of practice, Corina would comb out their wet hair and twist it into intricate braids.

In addition to her seven daughters, Corina was taking care of two foster babies. And when I went back to finish school after I had Luke, Corina babysat for me.

Having reared seven daughters and numerous foster children from infancy to childhood, feeding them, burping them, changing their diapers, toilet-training them, keeping them safe, Corina was an expert. She'd developed a way with babies and young children. She knew how to keep them in line without ever raising a hand to them or even raising her voice. Around Corina, they did what they were told. They slept when she put them to bed and ate what she cooked for them. They played happily in their play pen until it was time for Corina to lift them out and put them in their baby walkers.

She cleared all the furniture from her front parlor and let the babies roll around as they pleased. The babies would kick off in their bright-colored walkers, propelling themselves forward, backward or sideways with a push of their bare feet against the hard wood floor. Plopped in one of Corina's extra walkers, Luke joined the fun.

He was a natural, Corina said. He took to the walker immediately.

"Like a duckling takes to water," she told me one afternoon when I came to pick him up. "Some of my other babies, they just sit there for the first couple of times. But not Lil' Lukie. No sir, he started kicking his feet and moving that little car around no sooner had I put him in it!"

Luke started walking early – for a white baby. Corina's encouragement and the influence of the foster babies had a lot to do with it. Corina's foster babies were toddling around on their little brown square feet by the time they were ten months old. Luke was not quite eleven months when he took his first series of steps.

Corina was the kind of mother I wished I could be. Maybe if I were more like her, my father would change his mind and let me raise Tony. She made it all look so easy. Luke was an angel around her. But at home with me, he changed back to the little tyrant I knew so well.

Saundra

I couldn't help but notice that Corina's oldest daughter, Saundra, was beginning to pop out around the middle. She was wearing her belts higher and her belly seemed to grow fuller with each day that passed.

She had a soft-spoken, shy, but always pleasant way about her. She helped her mother take care of the babies and her younger sisters.

No one ever came out and said, "You know, Saundra's going to have a baby." It was woven naturally into the fabric of day to day conversation at the Williams. "When Saundra's baby comes, we'll have to buy another crib." Or "Saundra, don't you be movin' around that heavy couch in your condition. Just wait till your father comes home. He'll do it."

Corina and Jimmie never seemed angry or upset at their eldest daughter for being pregnant. And Saundra never seemed ashamed. On the contrary, she held herself straight and proud, her face was radiant, joyfully expectant.

House Party

When the baby was born, a little boy Saundra named Jalan, Corina and Jimmie threw a big party to celebrate. The older women played a card game called pitty pat in the kitchen. The men played poker in the dining room. The young people danced in the parlor while the children ran through the rooms and out to the backyard to pet the dog, then back through the house, to play stoopball.

Saundra introduced me to the father of the baby, a good-looking young man who was almost as shy as she was. He looked up from his sneakers just long enough to say to me, "How d'ya do, Miss Ann."

There was no mention of marriage. I gathered the baby's father wasn't in a position to marry and support a family just yet. Saundra still had a year to go in high school. So for the time being at least, Saundra and her baby would live at home.

There was no shame, no pretense, no cover-up. Saundra had a baby and babies are blessings. They celebrated all night long.

African Side-Neck

On Tony's fourth birthday, with Luke in tow, I took the subway to the Whitehall station and then the ferry to Staten Island. It was an icy cold day in late November. I bought Tony a turtle. Not just an ordinary turtle, but an African side-neck. I found it in a shop in Manhattan that specialized in exotic reptiles. The turtle I chose for Tony was solely focused on what was going on to the left of him. He seemed to have no interest in looking right or straight ahead.

Luke, now one and a half, wasn't a happy traveler. When he needed to sit still on the subway, he'd want to run up and down the aisle. But when it was time to walk, he would soon tire and cry for me to carry him. I always gave in to his demands.

I clutched the brown paper bag in my right hand, struggling to keep the bag from swinging, to protect the turtle inside. I could hear him sliding around in his plastic terrarium which I had wrapped in a thick blanket. A tote bag of toddler supplies – cookies, juice, napkins – was slung over my shoulder. I held Luke's hand in my left, coaxing him up the steep hill that led from the ferry to my parents' apartment.

The ice had formed a slick coating on the sidewalk going up the hill. No one had bothered to shovel or sand as yet for the icy rain was still coming down. It seemed that for every step Luke and I took forward, we'd slide just as far back. A fierce wind blew off our hats and I had to run after them. Bits of hail swirled in spirals around us, stinging our cheeks. Our faces were scarlet. Our noses dripped.

Luke cried for me to carry him, stretching his arms out to me in misery. I picked him up and carried him on my left hip, rearranging my load. But he wouldn't stay still in my arms. He was kicking, flailing his arms, furious at the ice, the cold. He wanted it to stop and when it didn't obey, he kicked harder, screamed louder.

Later that day, in my mother's kitchen, Luke and I watched Tony blow out the candles on his birthday cake. Before making his move, he had spent some time studying the position of the candles, deciding where he would begin, what pattern his trajectory of breath would take. When he was satisfied with his calculations, he drew in as much air as he could and, with cheeks puffed out like two rubber balls, extinguished the dancing flames.

"What are you going to name your turtle?" I asked when he lifted the blanket from the terrarium and discovered the African Side-Neck, under a plastic palm tree, peering back at him with its neck craned sideways.

As if for inspiration, Tony glanced around the room. His eyes lingered on the birthday candles now lying side by side on the kitchen table.

"Candle," Tony said. He named his turtle Candle.

I'm Your Mommy

I wasn't able to see Tony, be with Tony as often as I yearned to. There was always some obstacle to overcome – the trip across the harbor, my parents' distrust of me, my husband's reluctance to placate my parents, my father's refusal to let Tony live with us, Luke's constant demands.

But when I did spend time with Tony, I'd wait for the moments when Luke and I were in the room alone with him. Then I'd whisper to him, "I'm your mommy, Tony. I'm your mommy." Tony would smile sweetly and continue whatever game he was playing, whatever book he was reading.

My father wanted me to believe that in my situation, a truly good mother would relinquish her child willingly. It was selfish, childish to want him to know the truth.

I would build up my courage to face my father and tell him I wanted Tony to live with us. He would glare at me with his thick dark brows raised in a look of disbelief, as if to say, 'I can't believe you're even considering this.' Then he'd clear his throat and say, "You know, Ana, if you really love Tony and if you really want the best for him, you'd recognize that your mother and I can give him a better life." His voice would soften with tenderness as he spoke of Tony. I knew that he loved my son as much as he would have loved his own son.

His love for Tony overshadowed any love or compassion he might have for me. His tone would turn to steel as he continued, "And if you think for one moment that I would let Tony live under the roof of that madman you married, you'd better think again!"

He forbade me to say anything to Tony about being his mother. "If you want to see him, if you expect us to allow you into our house, you are never to tell him, you understand?"

Yes. Yes, I hear you, I thought. I understand what you're saying, but in my heart I'll never accept it. It will never change the way I feel for Tony. I am his mother. He is my son and nothing you do or say can change that.

Oh, Jill!

I was lying next to Erik on the double bed in our apartment on Clermont Avenue. I wasn't sleeping, he was. It wasn't his snoring that kept me awake. Something else was troubling me, an insecurity I couldn't put into words. I reached over and touched Erik.

"Oh, Jill!" he moaned. I pulled my hand away.

I didn't say, No, my name is Ann. Remember? Ann, your wife, mother of the young child asleep in the crib here in this bedroom. I didn't say anything.

Erik sputtered. The blooper had registered on the radar of his mind. He slowly dragged himself out of the mire of his unconscious.

"Oh, what am I saying? Ann, I meant Ann." He turned to me but I quickly spun my body around to face the wall. I wrapped my arms around my chest, pulled my legs up to my torso, made a tight ball of my body – a sealed, silent package.

I wasn't working at a regular job yet. I still played with the idea of substitute teaching. I had not yet admitted to myself that I wasn't teacher material.

I had subbed at the nearby elementary school a couple of times and had gone on a number of job interviews, but even though I'd been offered some full-time positions that sounded interesting, I felt Luke was still too young to leave with a babysitter all day, every day.

Erik and I were having a rough time coming up with the rent money, the grocery money, money to fix the beat up old sports car. So Erik took a second job - a Friday night job at an advertising agency doing paste-ups. He'd heard about the job from some friends of ours, Pratt students.

One of the students who did paste-ups to make extra cash on Friday nights was a young woman named Jill.

Homely, I thought when I first met her.

Not a threat, was my second thought.

Jill

Maybe Erik had seen his mirror image in Jill, with her sad, hound dog eyes and stringy, skinny hair that couldn't decide if it were brown or blond, hovering somewhere in between. Both Erik and Jill had thin limbs with bulbous knees and elbows.

Jill had a haggard look and rarely smiled. I knew very little about her except that she lived in a red brick apartment building on Clinton Avenue and was a fine arts major at Pratt where Erik and most of our friends had gone to school.

When I first saw her, I felt sorry for her.

Many years later, I heard from Erik that he'd bumped into Jill on the street in Manhattan. She was homeless, a bag lady, down and out. He'd felt compassion and arranged for her to stay with his aging father who lived in the Village and had just lost his second wife. He needed someone to look after him, to clean his rooms and cook his meals.

Erik's arrangement didn't work out for long. A week or two later while Erik's father was napping, Jill gathered her belongings, lifted the wallet from his jacket pocket, and walked out, not bothering to say goodbye.

The Red Brick Apartment Building

Early one Saturday morning, I woke up suddenly and realized Erik's spot on the double bed was still empty. It was four a.m. and he hadn't come home from his part time job. I lay awake, listening for the coughing of a car engine shutting down, the clinking of keys in the metal gate. I waited until it was officially morning. 7:00. The baby was awake. I paced back and forth, bouncing him in my arms. I dialed the phone number of Erik's friend, David Kramer, the one who had arranged the job for Erik.

"Hello, David? This is Ann. I'm sorry to be calling you this early, but I'm really worried about Erik. He hasn't come home yet. He hasn't called. Is he with you by any chance?"

"Hey, Ann," David's voice was thick with phlegm, groggy with sleep. "Erik? Here? Nope." He was too sleepy to stifle the yawn.

"Well," I said. "If you see him, tell him to give me a call, okay?" I put down the receiver without waiting for a reply.

Now I felt foolish calling David. Hadn't I known in my heart, my gut, where Erik was? And as sleepy as David was, I could tell that he, too, could figure it out.

I got dressed, fed the baby, changed his diaper and strapped him into his stroller.

"Hey, little baby, we're going for a walk."

I pushed the stroller to Clinton Avenue. In the middle of the block, parked right in front of the red brick apartment building where Jill lived, was Erik's black Triumph.

My heart was a hammer pounding in my chest, shouting at me, "See, I told you! I told you!"

I could have ripped out my heart and used it to bludgeon the two of them, lying in bed in that red brick building; two skinny, gangly, big-kneed bodies wrapped around each other. I could have pounded them together like veal cutlets, smashed them flat until you couldn't tell where one began and the other ended.

I stood outside the apartment building rocking back and forth with the pounding of my heart. I stood there until the baby started to fidget in the stroller. Then I spun the stroller around and headed down the street toward the playground. Walking fast, almost running. Luke squealed with delight. Like his father, he loved speed.

Later, when I told my friend Louise, she said, "Well, he could've at least had the decency to pick someone good-looking. It's a double insult, you know, when a man not only messes around behind your back but then picks someone ugly."

I vowed to get even with that wayward, screwball husband of mine. No, no longer a husband, I thought. Husbands don't act this way, husbands don't chase after art students and spend nights with them. "Husband" was too dignified a title to confer on a man who would do such a thing.

I wasn't going to waste my fury being angry at Jill because I already knew that if it wasn't her, it would have been someone else. It did not take me long to realize that I was only fooling myself with thoughts like: Erik would never lie to me. He loves me, he would never do that to me.

The Film

There were four apartments in our brownstone – one on each floor – connected by stairs.

Erik and the baby and I lived on the basement floor. Above us lived Rose Marie Paolillo, her son Dominic and Vinnie – a short, pasta-bellied man who used to hit Rose Marie and accuse her of being with other men if she came home late from work. As I rocked Luke to sleep, I could hear the crying and yelling going on above me. Vinnie never left the building. He always seemed to be in his pajamas.

Above Rose Marie and the mysterious fat man lived Hank Ames, a cinematography student. Hank was able to afford the apartment on his own. No roommates. His parents in Ohio must have been wealthy. Occasionally, a female would move in with him, but Hank was always able to call the shots. He didn't seem to be dependent on the girlfriend's rent contribution. He could break up with her, exchange her for a different female or live alone any time he pleased.

Hank had an inflated opinion of himself. He considered himself destined for great heights in the art film world. He walked around with an air of being famous even before he finished his first student film.

He asked me to be one of his starlets. He was working on his final project for school, a short film for the Pratt student film competition. With all the beautiful young students to choose from, he'd asked me to be the nude in the dream scene. I liked the idea that he thought I was attractive enough.

I said yes under one condition. I didn't want my face to be visible. I knew Erik would eventually see the film. We were friends of Hank's. And the student film festival was an event we'd surely attend.

So one day when Erik was at work and the baby was taking his afternoon nap, I climbed the stairs to Hank's apartment, took off my clothes and stretched out on a blanket on the studio floor, feeling weird and uncomfortable. Hank, fully clothed, chewed on a tooth pick while he peered at me through the lens of his camera. Examining me. It was beginning to feel like the doctor's office.

But with revenge as my motivation, I was able to get into the role of artist's model. Slowly, I turned my torso to the right, my legs to the left, forming a gently sloped mountain range with the curves of my body.

The payoff came a few weeks later at the film festival. I sat next to Erik knowing that he'd give special attention to Hank's film. I had to resist the urge to glance at him when the image of my naked body appeared on the screen. I wanted to catch the look on Erik's face, but I was afraid I'd give the secret away.

Afterward, as we walked down the aisle of the theater, through the lobby and out into the night, I sensed that Erik was regarding me with an inquisitive gaze. He said, "You know that nude could almost have been you … but her breasts were bigger," he concluded, before we'd turned the corner from Willoughby onto Clinton Avenue.

Doug's Drugs

When we had a little more money, we moved from Clermont Avenue to a brownstone on the corner of Clinton and Greene. My friend Melissa lived on the first floor with her husband and their little daughter, Kelly, who was Luke's age. Melissa had a younger brother named Doug who lived upstate.

That summer Doug came down to Brooklyn to spend a couple of weeks with his sister. He brought along his tall skinny blond girlfriend and a stash of LSD. They came dressed in brown suede fringed jackets and matching suede pants. Both wore brown suede moccasins.

One night after dinner, I left Erik with the baby and went downstairs to visit Melissa. When I knocked on her door, Doug told me Melissa and his girlfriend had gone out. He invited me in. We sat across from each other at the dining room table. He reached into the right hip pocket of his suede pants and said, "Hey, Ann. Let's swallow some acid. I've got these two pills here – one for you, one for me."

I wasn't sure. I'd heard scary stories about LSD.

I had been with friends who were tripping, Barry Epstein and his girlfriend, Gloria Pascale. Her father had been a prize fighter. The Pascale Kid was his fighting name. Gloria and Barry asked Erik and me to be there while they tripped. We sat on their couch like two spectators watching a show.

I remember thinking they were acting awfully silly. It was hard to figure out why they would be so interested in every little, ordinary object lying around their apartment.

"Oh, wow, look at this!" Rose said, holding out a Welch's grape jelly glass for Barry to examine.

Barry held it up to the light, peering at it as if it were a rare jewel. "Far out!" was his breathless response.

After an hour or so I was beginning to wish there was a TV we could watch. "Is it almost over?" I whispered to Erik. "Can we leave soon?"

"Shhhh, you'll ruin their trip!"

When they had enough of glassware and knickknacks, Barry and Gloria took their clothes off and began exploring each other's bodies.

"Okay, that's it. I'm outta here!" I said. Leaving Erik on the couch, I walked back home alone.

A couple of months later, Erik took LSD with his wild male buddies. They raced motorcycles under the expressway, gunning the engines, feeling power between their legs.

I was leery of LSD. All this talk about mind expansion, consciousness raising. I wasn't so sure it was for me.

But Doug was so sweet, so innocent, like the younger brother I always wanted. When I was six and my mother was pregnant, my father said prayers with me and my older sister each night. I prayed that the baby inside my mother's belly would be a brother. My sister prayed for a sister.

How dumb. I thought. What did we need another sister for? What we needed was a brother. But I could not convince her. She kept on praying for a girl.

My mother had a girl. When I heard the news, I figured my sister got her way because she knew how to be good. And I was, well, not exactly bad, but without even trying I got into trouble. Often.

When Doug held out a pill to me, I swallowed it. Quickly. Before I could change my mind.

Doug and I walked a couple of blocks down Clinton to the playground. We sat side by side on the swings and pumped.

I pumped the way my father had taught me when I was a small child. "Push me, Daddy, push me high!" I would cry. I was a big, solid child and he would tire of pushing me, so he taught me how to pump, to lean way back, stretch my legs straight out as the swing swung forward, then lean forward, with my legs bent as it swung back.

I started to notice that the dull yellow glow from the street lights was brightening. Bright yellow morphed into green, green into blue, blue into violet. The colors fanned out in rays, as if something mystical, something cosmic were about to happen.

I sat still in my swing, forgetting to pump as I stared at the lights.

This is great, I thought. This is going to be just great!

Too soon for me, Doug decided we should go home. I skipped happily beside him. Drugs were his field of expertise. I left the decisions to him. Doug did not know this. If he had, he might not have accepted the responsibility.

Maybe he decided we should go back so someone else could watch over me during my trip. Maybe I was getting too weird, dancing home with arms spread wide, spinning, then leaping down the street.

Home to Erik. Home to our white rug.

I see myself lying on the rug in the front room. Why am I lying here and who else is in the apartment? Luke is asleep in his bedroom. Erik is here next to me, but what happened to my younger brother? Is he here? Vague, shadowy people watch me struggle as Erik holds me down. I can't make out who they are.

Erik is a skeleton smirking as he holds me down. I am seeing him as he really is – a bare-boned skeleton jeering maliciously at me as I struggle to get up, to run away, out the door. No! Get away from me! I manage to get to my feet, but the skeleton runs after me, pinches my arm as he grabs me. I am repelled, sickened by his touch. I kick, bite, twist my body violently to unlock his boney grip. I break away and run toward the window. I must get away from this evil! If I don't, his depravity will surely corrupt me until nothing pure remains. I run to the window and am about to jump out. The skeleton comes from behind and locks me in his vice of bones, pins me down on the white wool rug.

I don't know how long this goes on – all night, maybe.

At dawn, I stumble into Luke's room. Luke has slept through it all. I touch his beautiful, sturdy two-year-old legs, loving them.

There is still life; there is still sanity.

Advice From Joan

Not long after the LSD trip, my friend Joan and I sat on the stoop outside the apartment while Luke played with his trucks on the small square of grass we called a front yard. More and more when she came to visit, I'd monopolize the conversation with details of yet another fight I'd had with Erik, another instance of his temper, his cruelty.

After the LSD experience, I couldn't look at Erik without seeing him as a leering devil. I couldn't bear being with him, being near him, sleeping beside him night after night. He had become physically repulsive to me.

"How could I have ever married him?" I wondered out loud.

Joan leaned closer and looked me in the eye, "You know, if it's really all that bad, maybe you should see a counselor."

Ashamed

The woman who interviewed me at the social service referral agency was probably only five or six years older than I. But with her hair pulled back, her wire framed glasses, and her air of authority, she seemed much older. I sat at a metal table next to her, feeling belittled and intimidated by her brisk manner. She asked me questions about pregnancies, about children, and scribbled notes as I answered. When I told her about Tony – "He'll be five in November" – my chest started to heave as if a volcano were about to erupt inside me. I started sobbing so hard I couldn't speak. The pain came in waves, made it difficult to breathe. I gasped for air.

I felt ashamed to have had a child without being married, ashamed that I had allowed my parents to take him, ashamed that I was now married to a man who did not want my child. I felt ashamed to be sobbing out of control in front of an unsympathetic stranger who just sat there watching me.

"Here is the name and phone number of a psychologist, Leonard Schutz," she said when I had regained a semblance of composure. "He will see you for an hour each week. And remember, if you decide he is not right for you and you would like to see someone else, feel free to give us a call."

Leonard Schutz

I never called him "Leonard." He was Mr. Schutz. Not Dr. Schutz, for he was not a psychiatrist. He was a psychologist, a therapist.

Mr. Schutz was tall and thin, long limbed and stiff. When I first saw him, my heart sank. He reminded me of Dr. Doyle. Were all therapists tall and thin? But Dr. Doyle' hair was brown; Mr. Shutz's hair was black. Too black, unnaturally black for his heavily lined, saggy jawed face. As he sat in the straight-backed chair facing me, I could imagine him thinking, What a crazy *shiksa*!

I must have been crazy to marry a wild, dangerous young man like Erik, a guy who could explode at any minute. Helen, his mother, used to say about Larry, one of Erik's old high school buddies, "He's a walking keg of dynamite, just waiting to go off." She could have been talking about her own son, with his violent rages, a guy who kicked, punched, threw heavy objects, a guy whose face, neck and back erupted in angry red bumps with white tips.

I must have known that Erik did not want Tony, had no intention of letting Tony live with us. Was my need to get away from my parents greater than my need to be with Tony? In Mr.

Schutz's office I cried for my lost child. I told him I wanted my son. I wanted Luke and Tony to be brothers.

When I was going to Mr. Schutz, Tony had started kindergarten. Luke was a fair haired, two-year-old who loved jumping up and down in piles of autumn leaves. I remember bringing two photos to show Mr. Schutz – one of Luke, one of Tony. The one of Luke was taken by Helen's husband, Dan, in their backyard in Great Neck. Luke's little round chin is almost completely hidden by the turtleneck of his red sweater. His face radiates delight as he scoops up handfuls of leaves and flings them to the wind. In the other photo, taken by my father, Tony stands outside a church, gazing solemnly into the camera. It's Sunday and he is dressed in a dark blue suit. His eyebrows, knit in consternation, are an exact replica of my father's.

I remember a dress that I wore when I went to see Leonard Schutz, a red and blue striped, sleeveless turtleneck dress, a form-fitting dress, not overly tight, nicely snug. I felt self-conscious in it, for my arms were bare and I wasn't so sure I liked my arms. They were kind of muscular like my Uncle George's – but he could make his bicep muscle jump up and down his upper arm.

It was the only dress I owned in those days. So even though I felt self-conscious in it, I wore it. And I discovered a funny thing: when I wore it, Mr. Schutz liked me more. His eyes stayed on me and he would say I was doing well, I was making progress, I was maturing, I was working out my life. When I wore jeans, he acted as if I'd had a setback.

I started to experiment and, sure enough, every time I wore the dress he seemed pleased with me. I wanted him to be pleased with me.

I remembered the woman at the referral agency telling me, "If you decide he is not right for you and you would like to see someone else, give us a call." But even though I felt uncomfortable with Leonard Schutz, even though I felt I was getting nowhere, I did not want to hurt his feelings. So I stayed with him.

Could anyone have helped me then? Could anyone have stopped the runaway train that was my life? I thought I was being a modern, progressive mother by letting Luke crawl wherever he pleased, get whatever he cried for, make scenes in department stores, monopolize my attention when my friends came over. I told myself I was allowing him to be a free spirit, but in reality I didn't know how to stop him; I didn't know how to quiet him down. And I'd get even more flustered, more embarrassed when others were watching and could witness my incompetence as a mother.

Mr. Schutz Meets My Father

I told Mr. Schutz my parents had bamboozled me. I'd been cheated out of my son. He decided that I should ask for Tony back from my parents. With his help, I might be able to convince them.

The one time my father came with me to see Mr. Schutz was all it took for him to realize that my father was a man whose mind was made up. A man who would not budge.

My father sat in an upholstered armchair that Mr. Schutz moved from its usual spot in the far corner to the center of the room, next to my chair. His elbows placed comfortably on the armrests, his hands loosely clasped in front of him, my father looked relaxed, dignified, even regal.

Seeing him there, I thought, "Leo. King of the Jungle." I had learned about Leos and their personality traits in the Sunday Herald Tribune. When I was a little girl in Westfield, every Sunday after church, my father would stop at the corner store to buy the paper. At home, I would spread out the cartoon section on the living room rug. First, I'd read all the funnies from Dondi, the Italian orphan, to Prince Valiant, then the horoscopes. I learned all about the astrological Sun signs and their qualities. I knew my father was a Leo.

I'm a Cancer – a crab. He's a lion. How can I ever expect to prevail? I wondered.

I heard Mr. Schutz saying to my father, "I would like to ask you to take a moment to look at this situation from the perspective of your daughter. She is Tony's mother, after all. She gave birth to him and like any mother, she wants her son to live with her, to grow up knowing that she is his mother. It causes her great pain to be denied her natural right to nurture her son."

My father listened intently to what Mr. Schutz had to say.

I thought I detected an involuntary flicker of an eyelid at the word "pain." But my father's voice was calm and controlled when, after clearing his throat, he said, "Mr. Schutz, you don't know my daughter the way I do. And you don't know her husband. Neither one is fit to be a parent." He paused for a second to make sure he had made his point. "As long as I am alive, I will never allow Tony to live with them."

Bad Girl

In his top dresser drawer, my father kept a magazine clipping of a photograph taken at a "pot party" near NYU. In the foreground, stood a dark-haired woman in a black bikini with her back to the camera. He was sure that it was me – no matter how loudly I protested, he was convinced I attended pot parties in a bikini.

I didn't even own a black bikini. And the woman in the picture was a good ten pounds heavier. Why couldn't he see that? Why wouldn't he believe me?

"Believe you? You're an inveterate liar."

Psychologists Made My Mother Cry

At least my father was willing to come and listen. My mother had been asked to come but she refused. Psychologists made her uncomfortable, made her cry. The few times she had been to see a psychologist turned into disasters.

When we first found out that I was pregnant, Lee's parents had arranged for me and my parents to speak with a psychologist who was also a pastor at their church. They had no intention of allowing their son to marry me – not that he wanted to – and hoped we could be convinced that giving up the child would be best in the long run.

Fixed minds, closed hearts. No one – neither my father nor my mother – was thinking, Maybe we could put our heads together and figure out a way to help our daughter keep her child.

The idea that I, the mother of the child, might be able to manage with some help, was never discussed. Accusations bounced back and forth from one side of the room to the other. Then my mother would cry and moan, and I would want to run to her side, cradle her narrow shoulders, stroke her soft, fine hair and say, Mama, don't cry, please don't cry. It's going to be all right. Don't worry, please don't worry.

Who was hurting more, who was the one to be pitied – my mother or me? My father suffered silently. He let my mother and me compete for the title of "most pathetic."

The only sign of his suffering was the tic in his right eye that caused it to wink involuntarily.

I wonder if anyone in his office sensed that he was going through a difficult time. I doubt that he ever told anyone what was going on, but what do I know? Maybe he had a confidant.

For a while, I was convinced my father had a lover, a girlfriend. I had seen a photo of her after Tony was born and my mother insisted that my father sell the house in Westfield.

During the time it took to sell the house and move out, my father rented an a large three bedroom apartment in Brooklyn where we would live – my mother, my father, my sister Sally, baby Tony and me, the pariah. But before moving his family in, I believe my father lived there with his girlfriend.

I spent the night in the apartment on the day before the movers came. My father was still at work and, not having much else to do, I started poking around, opening and closing the casement windows, checking out the kitchen cabinets, the bedroom closets. On the shelf in the bathroom off the master bedroom, I found a bottle of unfamiliar perfume and body lotion. On the nightstand beside the bed, I found a photograph of a middle-aged woman smiling sweetly into the lens of my father's Polaroid.

Mr. Schutz Meets Erik

I viewed the session with my father as a complete bust, and wished I had never brought him to see Mr. Schutz. Before, there had been an illusion of hope. Now the situation seemed bleak, but Mr. Shultz chose to look on the bright side. "Now we know for sure he understands your point of view. I was concerned that perhaps you had not made your desire to have Tony clear enough."

When Mr. Schutz gave up on my father, he tried to help me with my marriage. He asked me to bring Erik in to see him.

I'm not sure exactly what Mr. Schutz was going to talk to Erik about. Maybe he just wanted to size him up, get a first hand reading of this young man I'd so hastily married, this scruffy, arrogant young man. Arrogance based on what? Certainly not good looks, certainly not money, certainly not position in life. Erik's attitude was: attack before you are attacked, intimidate before they try to intimidate you.

Erik sat next to me in the upholstered chair, with his right foot propped on top of his left knee. I noticed that Mr. Schutz kept his gaze on that foot for a moment or two longer than one normally would. Although his face kept its neutral expression, I could almost hear him thinking, Damn, that's a big foot!

Mr. Schutz tried to engage Erik in a discussion about our marriage, but Erik talked about his job, his design projects. Puffing out his thin chest, he said, "I know more about design than those straight-laced, tight-assed architects I work for."

He got really excited talking about his plans to build a sailboat in the basement of our apartment building in Brooklyn.

"Oooh," he said leaning forward with both feet planted on the floor. "It's going to be a trimaran like the ones the Polynesians built almost 4,000 years ago. A sailboat with three hulls, a main one and two smaller ones."

Mr. Schutz listened politely.

I wondered if Erik's childlike enthusiasm was striking Mr. Schutz as strange and inappropriate. I thought of the time, several months back, when Erik bought a new, brown corduroy three-piece suit. He was so excited, so pleased with how he looked, that he went around the neighborhood wearing the suit, showing it off to his friends.

Just like a child, I thought, but then who was I to talk?

Erik was perched on the edge of the upholstered seat, elaborating on his subject, "As soon as I finish rebuilding the engine on the Triumph, I'll start on the trimaran. My dream is to load Ann and the kid into my boat and sail across the Atlantic."

Erik's dream was my nightmare. There was no way I would step foot on that boat. I sat in the straight-backed wooden chair, silently shouting, Help! God, somebody, please help me!

Erik rambled on about his projects. But when Mr. Schutz tried to get him to talk about our marriage, he clammed up.

Did I understand that Erik was unable to admit to any weakness, any trouble? I remember feeling terribly frustrated. I realized I would have to make my own decisions about what I needed to do. But how do you make decisions when you don't trust yourself?

Martha

Although I didn't have money to properly take care of a pet, I had several cats and dogs over the course of the four years I stayed with Erik. Erik liked cats – he'd grown up with them, he liked their detached, aloof attitude – but he didn't like dogs, and I imagine most dogs didn't like him.

Why then did I always say yes when a stray dog walked into my life, when a friend asked if I could take one of his dog's cute puppies?

I had said yes when Martha came to me as an irresistible puppy with a soft, faun-colored coat. Now she was a gawky adolescent, gentle with children but fearful of men. One day I had taken Luke to a birthday party for one of his friends who lived a couple of blocks away. We were only gone for a couple of hours. It was a weekend and Erik was working in a spare room set up as a woodworking shop with power tools – drills, electric saws, hammers; sharp things, heavy things, dangerous things.

When I came home, I found Martha shivering in the bathtub, blood streaming from her right front paw, forming a pool of red beneath her. Erik must have thrown one of his tools at her. I wrapped her paw in a bath towel and carried her down the hallway to the front door. I was on my way to the veterinary hospital on Myrtle Avenue, but before leaving, I called out to Erik, "You did this to her, didn't you?"

As I slammed the door behind me, I heard him mumble something about "that stupid mutt."

Sorting Things Out

After what happened to Martha, I had no doubts. I had to take Luke and Martha and get away from Erik. Fast.

I had a job as a receptionist at Pratt, and although my paychecks amounted to a mere pittance, not enough to rent a whole apartment, I had enough to rent a room.

I made an arrangement with our friend Ed, who was sharing a space with two other Pratt students on the top floor of our old building, 411 Clermont Avenue. He would move in with Erik on Clinton Avenue. Luke and I would move back to 411. We would take Martha with us.

Maybe Erik was fooled by my choice of words or maybe he was feeling a little sheepish about what he had done to Martha. Whatever the reason, he didn't make much of a fuss when I told him that I needed time "to sort things out" – whatever that meant. "Sorting things out" didn't sound so final, so serious. It didn't sound the way I felt: I was leaving and never coming back.

Part III

Kingston, NY

Tough

Being on my own was tough. I could barely afford enough for us to eat. When Luke needed new shoes, I had to swallow my pride and ask my father for money. Erik refused to help me out.

"If you can't take care of him, let him live with me!" he said. Maybe he thought I'd cave in and come back to him.

Never. I would never go back, but neither would I let Luke live with him. It was bad enough that Luke stayed with him every other weekend. I knew how reckless Erik was, how heedless of Luke's safety. I had witnessed time and time again how Erik seemed to enjoy putting him in dangerous situations.

Just a few months after I moved out, Erik sold the Triumph and bought another sports car – a red Riley roadster. One Sunday on my way down Clinton Avenue I saw Erik pass by in the red roadster sitting up tall behind the wheel, proud as a bantam rooster. Next to him was a young woman, and beside her, Luke, my son, my toddler, my baby, squeezed against the door of the old beat-up car, the door that might suddenly swing open as Erik rounded the corner, taking it fast, tires screeching.

Maybe Erik thought he was toughening Luke up, just the way his uncles toughened him up years ago. He told me that when he was still just a young boy of six or seven, his

Uncle Carsten, the most incorrigible of the three Swenssen brothers, threw an electric clock at him while he was standing in a puddle of rain water. "Here, kid. Catch!" Erik caught the clock and, jolted by the electric current running up his arm, immediately dropped it. The clock was still plugged into the outlet on the workshop wall. This was how Carsten taught Erik about electricity.

When Luke was with Erik, I feared for his safety, but Erik was Luke's father and, though I would have liked to, I could not break all ties with him. Luke adored him. He was furious at me for leaving his father and cried when he couldn't see him.

Divorce Papers

Two years had passed since I had packed my things, put Martha on a leash, picked Luke up in my arms and left Erik. I asked a couple of male friends if they would serve the divorce papers. But they were familiar with Erik and his trigger-happy temper. They didn't want to risk a punch in the nose. My friend Joan, on the other hand, knew that Erik would be happy to see her. He'd be excited by the sight of her long, blond hair and her large round breasts.

It was early on a Sunday morning. She had to knock on his door several times, but he finally appeared, dressed only in jockey shorts, his hair all greasy and flat. She shoved the divorce papers at him.

"Here, these are for you, from Ann," she told me she said. Then she quickly turned to leave. "Well, have a nice day!" She waved to him as she trotted briskly down the stairs. She said he stood in the doorway, dazed and confused, clutching the papers in his hand.

Erik thought that if he didn't respond to the summons and didn't show up at the courthouse, there could be no divorce. He was wrong. By not responding, he was tacitly agreeing.

Divorce

I sat in the witness stand in the Court House in Staten Island wearing a new dress – a wine-colored mini-dress with long, billowy sleeves. The skirt flared, so even though it was short, short, short as was the fashion in those days, at least it didn't cling to me. At least when I sat down alongside the judge to finalize my divorce, the flared skirt covered more leg than it would have, had it been pencil-tight.

My father was standing before me, asking me questions. My father, my lawyer. He was handling my divorce. I had no money for a divorce, no money to spare, so who could I turn to beside my father, the man who had told me so?

I suppose, if I had waited long enough, Erik would have eventually done something to legally end our marriage. But I had no intention of waiting. I needed to be the one to initiate the divorce. I needed revenge. I needed to hurt him. I needed to wield some power.

In those days in New York State, you had a choice of five grounds for divorce. I chose cruel or inhuman treatment. I could have chosen adultery but cruel or inhuman treatment seemed to sum it up nicely.

Yet as much as I thought I hated Erik, when the divorce was final and I handed him his copy of the decree, I noticed his hands shaking. The paper rattled. He was sitting in his car outside my apartment after dropping Luke off. I had to walk away to stop myself from reaching out to him.

Adoption

I was wearing the same wine-colored mini-dress when I returned to the Family Court a couple of months later for the adoption proceedings. My father and mother had decided to legally adopt Tony. A nagging fear kept them awake at night, the fear that I would take Tony away from them. They pressured me to agree to the adoption.

Once again my father was the attorney handling the case. To prepare me for this moment in the courtroom, he employed the reverse psychology he had used so many times as I was growing up. It had always worked. "I know you're going to disappoint us," he said, with an edge of disgust in his voice. "I know you'll never do what's right for Tony. You think only of yourself, never giving a thought to all that your mother and I have done for both of you."

I remember how the judge leaned towards me and in a warm, fatherly voice said, "You shouldn't feel pressured to give up your son. Don't do this unless you are absolutely sure it is the right thing to do.

"I am about to ask you a question. Your answer will have far reaching consequences, both for you and for your son. Before I ask you, I want to make sure you understand the consequences of your answer. If you answer yes to this question, you will surrender all legal rights to your son. If you say yes, you will give up forever – not just for one or two years, mind you, but forever – your rights as a mother to your son, Anthony."

I barely heard him ask me the question. My father had fixed his unblinking, Houdini-like gaze on me and wouldn't let go. My attention was dominated by those black, piercing eyes that always saw the worst in me.

For one brief moment, emboldened by the judge's words, I was about to cry out, No! My answer is no. I'm his mother, he's my son, they can't do this to me! Please don't let them! But with my father's eyes on me, threatening me, intimidating me, the words got stuck in my throat. If I said no, I would prove my father was right – I was an ungrateful, rebellious daughter who only wanted to bring shame and heartbreak to her parents. By saying yes, I would show my father I really was a good girl. I would show him that I never purposely tried to hurt him and I really did want what was best for my child.

Was I so naïve to believe that the offering of my first-born son would make my father approve of me?

"Yes," I said lowering my head. I pushed the mini skirt down as far over my knees as it would go one last time before I stepped down from the witness stand and left the courtroom.

Not That Bad

You tell yourself, This is bad, but not *that* bad. It's not denial. You're not denying that it's bad, you're just telling yourself it's not unbearable, it's not as bad as that.

What's "that"? You never ask the question because if you did you'd upset the apple cart. You'd flip that cart upside down. You'd pick those apples up one by one and fling them – at your father, at your mother, at anyone who would dare to take your child from you.

You might end up in prison or in a mental institution. No, it's best to tell yourself it's not that bad.

I Still Cry

Even now as I write these lines describing the courtroom scene, tears smudge the ink, wrinkle the paper. Recently someone who had read this story of Tony said to me, "You know, if Tony had been given a choice, he would have wanted to be with you, his mother."

Was this really the first and only time in all these years since Tony was born that someone suggested Tony may have wanted to be with me and not my parents?

Even if someone had said it to me sooner – a friend or therapist perhaps, never my mother or father, not even my sisters – I doubt it would have registered.

Although I dreamed of being with him, I never imagined he might prefer to be with me if he knew I was his mother. I was convinced I was a bad mother. Poor Luke had no choice, but Tony did. Why would he choose me?

Some nights I'd rock myself to sleep, lost in a fantasy: I'm sitting in a Queen Anne chair, wearing an expensive gown, my two handsome, well-dressed sons stand beside me – Tony on my right, Luke on my left. We are posing for a photo that will soon appear in the special Mother's Day issue of the New York Times *Magazine Section*. The whole world will know that I am Tony's mother and that Luke is Tony's brother.

Biological Mother

When Tony was thirteen, my father told him that I was his mother. Thirteen, the coming of age.

I picture them alone together in the kitchen. My mother is out shopping for groceries. My father had waited for a peaceful moment. No moments were peaceful around my mother.

"Have a seat, Tony, I want to talk with you." At thirteen, Tony is a boy scout, a straight A student. He plays the cello. Out of chubby, awkward pre-adolescence, a strikingly handsome young man is emerging. He takes the chair to the right of my father who sits at the head of the table.

My father clears his throat. He tells Tony that he has something important to say, something that he could not tell him before. Tony would have been too young to understand.

"Annabelle, whom you have known as your sister, is your biological mother. Aida, whom you know as your mother, and I adopted you when you were just a baby. Annabelle was very young when she gave birth to you. She was not able to take care of you."

He takes Tony's hands in his and continues, "We love you Tony. We love you as much or more than if you were our own son."

Lines of concern form between my father's thick dark brows drawing them closer. Tony sits motionless, silent. His brow is furrowed as well.

"Do you have any questions, Tony?" my father asks.

Tony hesitates, then shakes his head, "No, Dad."

Maybe this wasn't the great surprise that my father believed it would be. Maybe Tony knew all along.

Why do I Still Cry?

If I had thought that Tony might want to be with me, I believe I would never have given him up. But, what would his life have been like with me? Would he have gone to Princeton, then to the University of Chicago? Would he have earned a Ph.D. in Math, become a financial mathematician, married a lovely woman with a sunny disposition, adopted two little boys from Guatemala?

Knowing all of this now, why do I cry when I tell the story of my first child? Why does it still hurt when the ending is a happy one?

www.ingramcontent.com/pod-product-compliance
Lightning Source LLC
Chambersburg PA
CBHW042027050526
44107CB00103B/731